How to write a

What you must know about being a writer.

From gathering your ideas to getting your book published.

by

Vivian Venfield

Table of Contents

Table of Contents

Table of Contents

Table of Contents

Chapter 1) What You Must Know About Being a Writer

When you first get started with writing, you likely have all sorts of ideas about it. Writing has a profession has been obscured by romantic and dramatic stories, and the situation goes all the way back to famous writers like Edgar Allan Poe to the present day with things like the television show *Castle*.

Before you even sit down to write a book, keep a few of these important things in mind.

1) Writing Is Work

Writing is just as much work as digging holes in the yard or sitting down to fill in field after field of an Excel spreadsheet. It will have long periods of being tedious, where you feel as if you are just plodding from point A to point B, and there are plenty of days when you would just rather be hanging out with your friends.

For some people, writing is not work. It is a hobby that they can pick up and put down when they like. They can produce great things doing this, but if you are not willing to put in the work for hard bits, which include editing, submissions and critique, you are not going to be able to get your story out there.

Remember that if writing were easy, everyone would be doing it. The tricky issue is that for the most part, just about anyone can put words on paper or on the screen. This is just where writing begins, however. The work comes in when you are willing to do the tedious bits, and when you are willing to do the tedious bits as often as you are willing to do the fun bits.

2) You Are Not Going to Get Rich

Just about every writing guide says it, so the fact that it is being repeated here tells you that it needs to be said.

You are not going to be Stephen King or John Grisham. There are a lot of factors that go into being a successful writer, but there is no formula for being a wildly successful, famous one.

If you are good, hard working and a little bit lucky, you'll be able to make a bit of cash off of your work. You may even be able to make a living off of it, although this usually comes with publishing a lot of things, rather than one really good thing.

Accept the fact that you'd probably make more money working in an office and really assess whether you still want to do it. Write because you love it, but seriously think about what you get out of it.

3) People Don't Want to Hear About Your Book

You have to believe that your story is amazing. The bottom line is that if you don't believe in your work, no one will, and the sad thing is that at the beginning, no one is going to believe in it!

This is an overstatement. Chances are good that you know people who love your writing, but for the most part, most people don't want to hear it.

It's a little crushing, but this can keep you on track in a way. If you spend more time talking about your book than writing it, something is wrong.

4) There Is No Magic Formula

There are thousands of books out there that give you a formula for how to write a book, and there is something very appealing about them. It's very tempting to think that there is a step-by-step procedure to follow, where if you do so many words in one day or if you make sure that you hit the milestones of rising action, climax and falling action that you will have a best-selling novel on your hands.

The truth is that there is no one-size-fits-all solution for how to write your story. You can learn a lot of useful things about story structure and flow, but at the end of the day, every writer is different and every story is different.

There is no one way to write a story, and if you think there is, you are going to have a lot of problems.

The key is to find an approach that works for you, and chances are good that your own approach is going to be a combination of things that you pick up through trial and error.

5) You're Going to Hate It

The longer a piece of writing is, the more likely it is that at some point in the process, you are going to hate it. You are the person who is going to be the closest to everything in the story, and you will see every flaw, every problem, and every cheat that you used to get yourself out of a tight narrative spot.

Every writer has a moment or more where they hate what they have produced. This does not mean that you should to throw it out. There will never be a piece that you love from beginning to end, and if there is, there is likely something wrong with it.

You need to accept that your work will not always be pleasant to look at or to acknowledge that you made it, and that you will need to fight through it.

6) Writing is Solitary

You may think that you know this, but if you are writing, you are going to need time apart from other people. Even if you are someone who prefers to write with some background noise on in the background, you will find that writing, or at least, good writing, is something that separates you from other people.

Like any other creative endeavor, it will split you off from being social with people sometimes. Remember this if you are someone who thrives on seeing others and being part of a social scene. Your ability to be social will be at least a little curtailed if you are working on something on a regular basis.

There is no such thing as a writer who does not need an editor. It is very rare to find a writer who can edit their own work on their own. They do exist, but there is a reason that all major publishing houses have each and every writer work with an editor. For some projects, you need to be willing to talk with more than one.

Remember that the editor is there to help you and to make your work better. If they tell you to fix something, add something or remove something, it is to make the book better.

Of course, you can question them. You can ask them what changes are being made for what reason, and you can always argue your case. Save your arguments for the things that are most important to you, however. There is more on this topic in the chapter on editing, but in general, be willing to listen to your editors and to really hear what they have to say.

7) You Can't Please Everyone

Just like there is no perfect food, there is no story, novel, poem or narrative that is going to appeal to everyone. If you are lucky, you are going to be able to show your work to people who like it. They may fall in love with it and recommend it to their friends. It might change their life.

On the other hand, it is important to remember that there are also going to be plenty of people who don't care for it and even people who hate it.

Write your work for the people who do love it, and do your best to ignore the people who hate it. This is an important part of surviving as a writer and making sure that the critics don't get you down.

8) There Is an End

No novel lasts forever, and in its own way, this can be quite comforting. Eventually, all writers start thinking about the word count, whether they are putting together a little 20,000 word novella or a 200,000 word epic.

However, at the end of the day, the novel is just words put together in an order that no one has ever seen before. There is a finite end to it, and you will not be doing it forever. This can keep you going as you slog through the tedious bits.

9) It's Going to Be Fun

It might surprise you to read this given everything that's come before, but writing your story is fun. In fact, it can be some of the most fun you know how to have.

Writing can remove you from yourself and put you right in the middle of a world where anything is possible.

If you are going to write, make sure that you have a good time.

Chapter 2) Gathering Your Ideas

Every piece of writing starts with an idea of some sort. It might be an idea that you have had for a long time, or it might be an idea that just came to you out of the blue.

An idea can be as simple as "I really want to tell the story of how my grandparents met and fell in love," or as complex as "I wonder how the world would change if half of the population was suddenly rendered blind and the other half deaf."

These are both great ideas, and their worth as stories will only come through when you write them down. In the early stages of writing your story, however, there are a few things that you need to remember with regards to your ideas.

1) Write Them Down

Some people keep a notepad on them at all times, while some people use a voice recorder to keep track of the random ideas that they have.

Just because you write down an idea does not mean that you need to do something with it. As a matter of fact, a lot of ideas that get written down are just as easily discarded.

However, writing something down makes it seem more real and more tangible. When you have written something down, you can see where it is going to go and you can make it something to hang words off of. If your stories just stay in your head, you will find that they never get anywhere.

Writing down your ideas gives you a great first step when it comes to getting started.

2) Consume Media

There is a phrase in programming that could just as easily describe writing, and that phrase is "garbage in, garbage out." This means that if you only have bad input, your output is going to be something similar.

You don't get good results by using bad code, and you don't get good writing by consuming "garbage."

This does not mean that you have to limit yourself to only the finest music and novels, at all. This saying just wants to remind you that the work that you produce will always be affected by what you are reading and watching yourself.

There is always going to be something of what you watch and read in what you write. It might be a random fact or it might be a tone, a turn of phrase or even an attitude.

When you are writing, make sure that you consider what you are doing to influence it. Think about your sources and think about what you are consuming. This can help you stay on track.

3) Diversify, Diversify

If it's good for an investment portfolio, it is good for your writing. They say that there is nothing new under the sun, but the truth is that people who are saying that are thinking too broadly. There are plenty of elements that stories have in common, but when you get down to the narrow details, there are plenty of things that never get talked about.

When you look at the classics of Western literature, for example, an observant eye will quickly notice that the race that figures most predominantly is Caucasian, and that most of the writers are male. This may be the widest demographic published, but it is a limiting viewpoint.

Be willing to explore outside of your comfort zone and to make sure that you are taking a look at things from every angle. Consume media from a wide variety of sources, and be willing to go out of your way to learn something new.

4) Explore the World

They say that you should always write what you know, so make sure that you know a lot! When people think of writing what they know, they often become discouraged because they feel their lives are boring.

The thing to remember is that your life is only as boring as you allow it to be. Not all of us can be world travelers, but there is a good chance that you can sign up for a class, talk to someone through the power of the Internet or simply get to know something that you didn't know about an obscure era of history.

What interests you, and what do you think would enrich your life? If you think that something is worth doing and worth writing about, chances are good that you can convince other people that it is interesting enough to read about!

Getting into a little more of the nitty-gritty of exploring the world, research for writing can be considered a tax write-off. If you have an accountant, be sure to discuss the matter with them, but in general, at least a small amount of the money that you invest in your writing can be written off at the end of the fiscal year.

5) Understanding Truth That Is Stranger Than Fiction

Just because something is true does not mean that it is good fiction. There are plenty of people who have told entirely true stories that get criticized for being too fantastical, too coincidental, or simply too clichéd.

They often feel very offended by this idea, because, after all it did happen to them! How could something that really happened be considered too wild for fiction?

In the first place, most people have a tough time believing in amazing coincidences and happenings that are too lucky. When it comes to writing, you can largely have coincidences that interfere with the character's life or that move the plot forward, but you should not have coincidences that are just too good for the main character. Most people read that as wish fulfillment and have a tough time buying into your story.

When you are thinking about how to make sure that your novel is realistic, take a moment to consider how the happenings fit. If the use of a real-life detail makes your narrative too unwieldy or if it creates a situation that is altogether too convenient, leave it out of a fictional work.

This is of course thrown out for a factual recounting of an incident that happened to you or to someone that you know. Present the facts calmly, and let them stand. In something like a memoir or a biography, you will discover that things are almost easier to sell as actually happening.

6) Be Open to Things

Inspiration is all around us. Even if you have a story idea in mind already, be willing to keep your ears and eyes open and to listen to other sides of the story.

Never do your research from just one side. For example, if you were writing an account of the Battle of Gettysburg, you would not write the story just from the view of the Confederates or the Union soldiers.

Instead, you would take a careful look at both sides, what happened and how they reacted. This is the only way to get a full account of what really happened.

In the course of writing down your story, you will find that the more information you have, the better off you will be. Look for alternative viewpoints and be willing to accept that the story that you are telling might end up being a lot different than what you started out wanting to create.

If you are writing a biography or a memoir, you likely know all about the life around which you are basing it. However, how much do you know about the time frame?

For example, if you are thinking about writing the biography of a relative who lived during the Depression, you might know that they lived in Kansas City. Do you know what Kansas City was like at the time?

By reading up on the city and the world that they were living in you will be able to create a much more engaging narrative.

7) Think About How Much Help You Need

When you are getting started with writing a book, there are going to be plenty of people around who want to help you and who have great ideas for you.

The thing to remember is that for the most part, you are best working on your own. Only get into a writing partnership with someone whose work you respect and who is willing to put in as much time as you.

Simply saying that you've got plenty of ideas is often enough to help people get the point.

8) Save Some for Later

When you are getting started on your very first writing topic, you will discover that there is a lot going through your mind. You might want to write a story that is meaningful to everyone, and you want to make it a romance, or a political thriller or an exploration of modern alienation. These are great things to write about, but make sure that you are doing your topic justice.

There are too many people who want to fit everything into one single book. Although there are some mash ups that are terrific, you'll find that more often than not, it is better for you to pick one thing and to focus on it.

Do not think that you have to put everything that interests you into one project. Think about the information that you have and consider whether it would be better in one book, or even two or three.

The more you put into a book, the more you have to explain, so be willing to divide up the information that you want to put out there.

This is something that can make a big difference to your plans so think hard. What does your project want to be? Do not slip in information or content just because it makes you happy. The first thing that you must always do is serve the story!

For example, think of the movie *Shaun of the Dead*. This quirky movie is the story of a man who wants to get back together with his girlfriend. It focuses on how he feels about her and just how he handles his life. The twist is that most of the action is taking place during the zombie apocalypse! Now if the movie had tried to be a quirky romantic comedy while also being a dire horror movie about the living dead, it probably would have flopped.

Instead, it's a bit of a cult classic these days. The writers made the right move by focusing on the small story of Shaun's relationships, both with his ex and with his best friend. That story is always front and center, and things like hoards of shambling undead are simply incidental.

When you go to write your novel, remember that you should keep your scope limited. There are a few writers who can do anything and everything. Malcolm Gladwell, for example, does very well as a generalist, but most of the other writers out there find that focusing on one thing gives them the clarity that they need.

9) Talk to Others

Part of being a great writer is being able to come up with your own ideas. However, no one does anything in a vacuum, and your writing is meant to be read. You can say that you are writing stories for yourself, but you should also consider how they look to other people as well.

Run your ideas by other people, and see what they have to say. If one or two people tell you your idea is bad, ignore them.

However, your friends can be very helpful if you have created a plot that reminds them strongly of the most recent movie blockbuster that you might have missed, and they can help you refine it.

No one is alone, and you will find that when you are putting together a book, you need help. Writers are people who function in their own heads a great deal, and this is something that can actually hurt you early on in the process.

Be willing to talk to others and to get their ideas. While you should always stay relatively independent about what you are doing, you should also think hard about how you can get the right kind of input.

10) Perfecting an Elevator Pitch

When you are looking to refine your work, consider putting together an elevator pitch. An elevator pitch is an advertising term that allows you to describe your story in the length of time that it takes to ride an elevator, and it is designed to help you take advantage of a fortuitous meeting with someone who can further your career.

Think about your story and see if you can describe it in two seconds. You do not have to give away the plot or name the characters, just come up with a very short description of it. If you are not sure how to proceed, try to come up with two sentences for a media property that you are familiar with.

For example, if you need to create an elevator pitch for the first Star Wars movie, it might go something like, "A young man comes of age under the tyrannical rule of an intergalactic empire. A tragic occurrence forces him to ally with smugglers and aliens as he comes to realize the truth of his mythic heritage."

Keep your elevator pitch short and sweet, and use it to direct your writing. Remember that your writing needs to be interesting to you before it can be interesting to every one else, and the elevator pitch is perfect when you are looking at how to make your story sound great!

11) What Do You Want to Read?

If you are someone who loves to read, have you ever noticed that there are stories out there that you want to tell? As you read more and more, you come to see that there are certain stories that happen over and over again, and some stories that never get told at all.

One of the greatest pleasures that we can enjoy when we read is to see ourselves reflected. If you do not see a reflection of yourself, it can be quite disappointing. This is something that drives many people to read, and it is something that can drive many people to write as well!

Think about the experiences that make you unique, and think about how they can translate to the rest of the world as well. Do you have a story that needs to be told? Do you know a story that is going to make someone smile or cry?

Remember that there is a very big publishing industry out there. Even if you do not have material that would be picked up by a major publisher, you will find that you might still have something that can be picked up by a small press or independently published.

Think about the stories out there that really spoke to you, and make sure that you consider what you want told to the world.

Many wonderful stories out there got told because the writer said, "no one tells this story, so I shall!"

12) Free Writing

Sometimes, your mind is buzzing with so many ideas that it can be hard to really sit down and determine what you are doing. You may find yourself starting to write but getting distracted.

Do yourself a favor and simply start by writing down everything that you have in your head. Sit down with a piece of paper and a pencil or open up a fresh Word document and start typing. Everything that you want to write about goes on this page, and it can be as specific as "older woman fights dystopian government" or as general as "coming of age as homosexual."

Get all of those ideas onto the paper and start by figuring out which of those ideas go together. There are people who do this exercise and end up realizing that they have enough material for half a dozen novels!

13) Understanding Length

Look at all of the material that you are thinking about writing and think about how much it will come to. A short story can be anywhere from 100 words to upwards of 10,000 words. After that point, up to about 40,000 words or so, you are in the territory of novels.

Most novels are between 60,000 to 100,000 words, with some going even further than that. As you write, start thinking about what you think you can see and how much space you need to fill. Some people prepare to write a novel and find that they've got enough for a short story and vice versa!

Chapter 3) Outlining

Your story needs to have a structure, and that is where a good outline comes in. If you think of your writing as a journey, your outline is your map and your itinerary. It tells you where you need to go, how long you need to stop there, and what you should do while you are there.

Some people can just plunge into a story and write from beginning to end, and if this works for you, by all means do it. An outline lets you lay all of your thoughts out before you need to commit, and it also lets you do things like set situations up at the right time and to put in foreshadowing if you wish to.

1) Basic Novel Structure

According to most Western conventions, there are five parts to any novel or story. These parts include exposition, rising action, climax, falling action and denouement.

Although many stories fit into this structure, not all of them do. Some stories move at a very slow and measured pace, using rhythm and common knowledge to build a very subtle narrative. Other stories use an alternating rising action and climax structure where every climax is a buildup to the grand finale at the end.

If you are interested in writing a story of any sort, whether it is a memoir, a science fiction thriller or a romance, it is a good idea to know what these five parts are and what they mean.

2) Exposition

Exposition is basically where you tell people what is going on and what they can expect. Depending on the story that you are telling, your exposition phase can be quite short.

When you are telling a story about your family, for example, you will naturally tell the listener or reader about who is involved, a little bit about what they are like and a little bit about the world they were living in.

If your story starts in the Depression, you may introduce everyone by relating an incident that demonstrates what their lives were like and how they were dealing with things.

Everything that you do at the beginning of a work should let people know what they are getting into and who they are going to be spending time with.

For example, this is where you are going to be describing your characters. You will need to talk about who they are, what they are like, what they want and how they are moving ahead with their lives.

Remember that there is no right or wrong way to describe your characters and their situation; there are only ways that are more or less elaborate. For example, the famous writer Ernest Hemingway was known for his extremely short, extremely staccato method of describing things. He wasted no words regarding what he wanted people to see.

There is no doubt that Ernest Hemingway was an important writer, but then remember that Edgar Allan Poe is another man who we consider to have shaped modern literature. His prose is lavish, and he spends long passages telling us where we are and what we should be looking at.

Decide on the tone for your work, and remember that you should just write naturally. When you go to describe your protagonist, make it as natural a thing as you can. You'll be surprised at how far your descriptions can go if you are careful with what you say.

Also remember that when it comes time to describe your main

character, do not do it by having them stand in front of a mirror. This is an extremely tired trope, and it has been done over and over again.

One exercise that might help you learn exposition is to think about it as an introduction. You are getting everyone into the story. Think about your favorite book or your favorite novel, and think about an iconic scene.

Write a brief paragraph that talks about what is going on in the scene and think of yourself as easing someone into it. Introduce someone to your favorite scene and try to make it as appealing as possible.

3) Rising Action

The rising action portion of a conventional story is one of the longest sections that you are going to need to deal with. This is where "everything happens."

Once the exposition is over, you will start your characters off on what they are meant to be doing. In a standard fantasy novel, for example, the rising action may begin when the heroine realizes that she is the secret queen of the country and must begin her quest for the throne. In a romance, the rising action begins when the hero and the heroine meet, starting off their romance. In an action movie, the rising action begins when the hero realizes that he needs to take steps to fix what has gone wrong.

Rising action is something that is a little tricky for some people to understand. They think that it is something that needs to be a steady buildup to the climax, but the truth is that it can be bumpy and not altogether even.

For example, consider the novel *Gone With the Wind*. The novel's headstrong protagonist, Scarlett O'Hara, goes through many changes of fortune. She marries, she is widowed, she loses a child, and she takes desperate risks to protect her home. During one iconic section of the text, she must run away from the burning of Atlanta.

Now, for most people the destruction of a large city is a fairly important event. In other books, it would definitely be the climax. However, in *Gone With the Wind*, the battle serves as an important background to Scarlett's life and the things that will make her into the woman that she is.

Do not think that you have to stack events one after another until you get to an event that is bigger and more important than all of them. The rising action should resolve naturally and gracefully in the climax, and that does not mean that it needs to be a steady climb.

Instead, some works are dependent on the rising action being quite subtle. Other works have the rising action as being something that stops and starts, creating a feeling of tension in the reader.

The way that you choose to handle rising action is up to you. All that you need to remember is that it must serve the story. Do not force action into your story where it feels like it does not belong. Go with what feels natural for the story that you are trying to tell.

Pick up some of your favorite books and some books in the genre that you are writing for. Look for the spot when the exposition ends and when the rising action begins. Trace the rising action until the climax, whatever that might be. This can teach you a lot about how some of your favorite writers structured their stories.

4) Climax

Some writers call the climax the pay off, and that is a good way to think about it. It can be said that writers make a bargain with their readers. They state that if the readers are willing to come along for the length of the story, there is a satisfying resolution waiting for them.

The climax is the strong point of the story, and it provides your readers with a satisfying conclusion for the action. For example, in a standard fantasy story, the climax occurs when the hero faces the villain and puts an end to their evil. In a romance novel, it is when the hero has saved the heroine, and they declare their love for each other.

Do not think that the climax is when you need to resolve everything. There are some stories that benefit from having everything tied off in a neat package, while there are other stories that benefit from having things trail off. Some people state that, for a realistic story, the climax only solves the main issue. Real life is sloppy, and all of our questions are never really answered, and some people feel that good writing should reflect this. Once again, this is something that is up to you. Just make sure that you make the choice deliberately.

It is a good idea to have your climax in mind when you begin the story. This is the point that you are working towards, and it holds true no matter what genre you are writing in.

For example, you are writing the story of a relative's life. The story begins with their birth, goes through what happened to them, and can climax with their death. Depending on the story you are telling, the story can also climax when they have achieved a dream, when they retire or when they finish a phase in their life.

The most important thing about the climax is that the audience must not feel cheated. This does not mean that you have to give them what they expect, but they must feel as if there is a point to the thing that they have read.

One example of a climax that defies expectations can be found in *The Wonderful Wizard of Oz*, by Frank L. Baum. In this story, a lot of the action seems to be building up to the meeting of Dorothy and her friends with the great wizard.

However, when they actually arrive in the city, they are met with bluff and bluster that inevitably ends up being a trick set up by a con artist. At this point, the audience is confused, and if the story had ended there, they would have had a right to feel cheated.

On the other hand, Dorothy and her friends are instead sent off to deal with the wicked witch, who has been lurking in the back of the story in many ways. Dorothy's story is not finished when she meets the wizard, but instead when she battles with the wicked witch.

Think about what you set up in the story. If you do not resolve it in the climax, you are effectively cheating your readers. This is something that can bring down a work that was otherwise very well written, so be willing to think extensively about what kind of work you are creating.

When you are in the position to consider the climax of your story, always remember that it must make sense with regards to the rest of the story, and it must deal fairly with your audience. If it does not do these things, your story has flaws that you need to resolve. Be willing to try on a few different climaxes just to see what happens. As a writer, you can experiment with the ending of your story.

5) Falling Action

Falling action is a relatively short section in your book, but it is still an important part of the process. After your readers have gotten through the climax, they need a certain kind of relief.

When you are looking for examples of falling action in great works of literature, think of the famous Shakespearean play, Hamlet. The climax of the play occurs during Hamlet's duel with Laertes, where treachery is uncovered and most of the cast ends up dead from poisoning or blood loss.

The falling action of the play is the quiet scene where a dying Hamlet refuses to allow Fortinbras to commit suicide, and instead asks him to stay alive to tell the entire sad story. After the frenetic action of the duel, the audience needs a short amount of time to recuperate.

Some people say that the falling action sequence is designed to let the audience exhale. If your climax kept them on the edge of their seats and had them holding their breath, falling action is when they can utter a sigh of relief, whether it is sad or happy.

6) Denouement

Denouement is a classic French term for the action that occurs after the climax and the falling action. In this area of the text, you work on what comes afterwards. You've put all of your effort into the rising action and the climax, and now you need to answer the question that should be on all your reader's lips; "well, what happens next?"

Some writers like to put a lot of detail into the denouement, while others like to give very little at all. In a fairy tale, for example, the entire denouement that is given is the iconic line, "they lived happily ever after."

A denouement does not mean that you need to promise everyone a happy ending, far from it. It simply puts the characters in a place where the readers are comfortable leaving them. For some narratives, it means that the main characters are off to start a family, while in others, they are setting off on another adventure. In some stories, it means that they are going to continue to use the things that they learned over the course of the stories. In other stories, it means that they are going to start to heal from the events of the story.

One of the most famous denouement sequences in the English language speculative fiction can be found at the end of the Lord of the Rings trilogy. After Frodo drops the ring into Mount Doom, he returns home. He lives for a few years in the shire, but eventually, he comes to the realization that he must travel west with Gandalf and the elves. These pages are short compared to the bulk of the rest of the work, but they are essential. They tell us that Frodo's story did not end with a comfortable normal life in the Shire. Instead, he felt a need to journey to the west and find something different.

Tolkien's denouement also tells us about how the lives of all of the characters we have come to care about play out. He talks about how they live and the place that they take in the world. While he could have ended the story with the success of the mission to drop the ring in mount doom, he chose to give us something more fulfilling. He gave us the idea that after the adventure is done, there is a life that can be returned to, and that some people do not return as whole as when they left.

In more recent literature, when the Harry Potter series ended, J.K. Rowling created an epilogue that showed where the characters ended up years in the future. She shows the main characters and their lives, and she mentions some of the supporting characters that the audience had become close to.

Some people love a great denouement, and some people feel that they are unnecessary. The route that you choose is entirely up to you and what you feel is appropriate for your story.

7) General Outlining

One great way to outline your story is simply to start with the structure that was listed above. On a piece of paper, draw five boxes and label each box with the five sections of the story.

Then simply start listing events as they occur in the story, grouping them where they would end up. This gives you a concrete map to follow.

8) Cloud Outlining

When you want to work with something a little less structured, take a moment to consider cloud outlining. A cloud outline is a very simple process that can help you organize your story.

Start with an empty sheet of paper. Think about the events of your story and write them down at any spot on the paper. These events can be in any order. They can be things that you know that you want to happen in the story, or they can be things that you are fairly sure that you want to happen in the story, or they can be things that you are still wondering about.

Draw circles around each event. Then simply draw arrows from event to event. Start with the earliest event on the piece of paper and draw an arrow to the next event. When you cannot go from one event to the next, that means that you need something in between.

9) Note Cards

One interesting way to outline your story is to simply put down every story element on a note card.

Buy a standard pack of note cards and start using them to take notes. Write down different characters, different places, and all of the events that you want to take place in your story. This can help you organize your thoughts, and it allows you to have your thoughts close to hand as you write.

When you want to use the note card method to organize your thoughts, clear out a space on the floor or on the table and start ordering your note cards according to how you want your story to go. Lay them out in order and allow yourself to consider how it all fits together.

When you see the information all laid out like this, it becomes very easy to figure out what might be missing and what you might need to do in order to make the entire sequence work.

10) Timeline

A timeline is not exactly an outline, but it also serves as an organizational tool. A timeline essentially traces the arc of your story in a chronological fashion, and it can be a good way to allow you to see what is going on.

Simply pick up a long strip of paper, whether it is a strip of receipt paper or a roll of butcher's paper, and start writing on it. Describe the events in the order that they happen, and soon you will see how easy it is for one point to lead to another.

Do not feel that your timeline needs to be dull. Instead, take a moment to color code it, to draw handy diagrams, and even to decorate it if you wish to do so.

If you have an area of your home that is dedicated to your writing, consider pinning the timeline up on the wall. This allows you to have a physical reminder of the events where you can see them and access them easily.

In many cases, the bigger the paper, the better. This allows you to make changes as you need to and to create the notes that allow you to figure things out for the future of the story.

11) Thinking Through Plot Points

Sometimes, when you are outlining, you can get stuck. You might not know how to kick events off, or you might come to a point where you are unsure how things are meant to proceed.

This is an interesting form of writer's block that occurs long before you have done much writing at all, but it can really stop you in your tracks.

If this is something that you have run into, take a moment and take a deep breath. Getting stuck can be quite uncomfortable, and you may find that it makes you feel a little panicked.

When you get stuck like this, simply start throwing solutions and what-if statements at the situation.

One example might be that you have two characters that are trapped in a small room. They are resourceful characters, but you do not know how they are going to get out without making the situation look ridiculous.

You can brainstorm all sorts of interesting ideas. Think about having an unlikely person coming to rescue them, or having one of them capitalize on a talent that was previously mentioned. Consider how people have gotten out of locked rooms in the past and be willing to experiment.

When you get stuck on an outline, always be willing to try lots and lots of different solutions. This is something that can help your writing get a lot more thorough while giving it a strong foundation to build upon.

12) Organize

When you are writing your story, remember that organization is key to swift writing. Keep your outline and your notes close to hand. Chances are good that as time goes on, you will no longer need them.

You'll know all about the plot points and the events, and you will not need to worry about what happens where. Despite this certainty, though, do keep notes.

The longer a story is, the more you are going to need to think about it. The more balls you will have in the air, and the more events you are going to need to juggle. You will forget things, and you may realize that you have written yourself into a corner.

Make sure that you do not have to do story structure work more than once. You wrote things down for a reason, so make use of them. Keep your notes in a little storage folder where you can see it, leave them on the computer in an email, or even tack it up on your wall.

Having all of your outlines available can help you get a general feel for the entire experience. If you change one event, you will be able to look at your notes and see quickly how things might change.

Many people are very visual when it comes to structure, and having the entire structure of your novel laid out for you is something that can help you move forward at a good pace.

Chapter 4) Research

We touched briefly on the idea of research in the chapter about gathering your ideas, but this important part of writing requires its own chapter.

The bottom line is that the more research you do, the better off you are going to be and the better your novel is going to end up. There is absolutely no shifting this. Unless you know your subject inside and out, you need to do your research before you start to write.

Some people begin to write and do their research as they go along, but this is something that can have some severe problems down the line. The last thing that you want is to hang a plot point off of a type of machine that didn't exist at the time or to send your characters to a town that was called something different or even non-existent when the story took place.

1) The Internet

The Internet is a great place to start. Wikipedia is a fantastic source for information, but the thing to remember is that this is an encyclopedia that can be edited by anyone. There is a lot of information out there, but you always want to confirm it through a scholarly source.

Check Wikipedia's footnotes, which can take you to actual scholarly articles that can flesh out your reading, and also spend some time reading on Google Books, where you can find a lot of texts that are no longer in print.

If you are writing a story where there is a lot of information needed on past eras and factual occurrences, it is going to be worth your while to get an account with a site like JSTOR, which houses a wide variety of scholarly articles.

Depending just on the popular articles out there gives you a good start but you will largely find that for a complete understanding of the topic, you will need something a little bit more precise.

Remember that the content on the Internet can be created and edited by a wide variety of people, and go to every source as a skeptic until you discover otherwise.

2) Personal Interviews

One of the best things that the Internet has done is that it has made the world a lot smaller. This means that you can find out about people researching the very thing that you are interested in and that you can see if they are willing to talk to you.

If you have a question about ancient Roman customs, you can email your questions directly to an expert, whether that person is a professor at a local college or a historian.

When you are addressing your questions to someone, remember to be polite. Introduce yourself, let them know what it is that you are doing, and ask them for help. You may ask them if they are comfortable answering questions for you and if they have the time to do so.

Do not be rude if you do not get a response, and if they do respond, thank them for taking the time. There are a number of people out there who would love to share their information in a specialized field with you, and this is something that can make a huge difference to your work.

3) Run and Find Out

Run and find out is the motto of the mongoose family from Rudyard Kipling's tale, "Rikki Tikki Tavi," and it's a good motto for writers too.

No matter what you are writing about, chances are good that you can really benefit from taking a trip if you can. When you are writing a memoir for yourself or someone that you love, head to the places you mentioned. Even if they have changed a great deal since the time of the events you are describing, it can give you a better idea of how things occurred.

If you are writing a story about a museum, visit the museum in question. If you are writing a thriller featuring the capital, see if you can take a trip.

The more time you spend investigating the area that you are writing about, the more likely it is that you will get the answer right. A lot of writers write about their hometowns, firstly because they love the town, but secondly because it is so easy to learn about it and what makes it distinct.

Your research gets a lot trickier when you are writing about things on the other side of the world or when you are considering talking about things that happened hundreds of years ago.

Do your best and use the Internet as a resource. Look up images of the places that you are writing about and make sure that you know what people are saying about it. Google Street View can be quite handy as you look for small details that make your story pop.

When in doubt, do what you can to interview people who have lived or worked in the area that you are writing about. Be willing to ask questions, but of course always be polite.

You might also be surprised at what you can learn through hands-on methods. There are plenty of places that will give you some quick and dirty training on nearly any topic you want to learn about, whether you are interested in tending to horses or learning what the life of a village blacksmith was like.

The more experience that you get on a certain topic, the more authoritative your writing is going to sound. Living historical events can teach you a lot about how people did things, and do not underestimate the enthusiasm of a hobbyist who wants to tell you all about their passion!

4) Avoiding Redundancy

One thing you should consider is researching whether anyone has had the same idea as you do! This mostly pertains to issues like writing speculative fiction and literary fiction, but it is worth checking around in general, especially if you have an ambition of selling your work to a conventional publisher.

Just take a moment to look around and to see if anyone is doing something similar to what you are doing. This does not mean that you need to scrap your idea if someone out there is doing a version of it, you just need to make sure that your version offers something that theirs does not.

Run a general plot outline of your work past some of your reader friends, and ask them if they have heard of something similar. When you are enchanted with a certain idea or a certain concept, it can be deflating to realize that you have basically recited the plot of *Star Wars* or *Titanic*, but it is a necessary realization to have, especially if you can get it at the beginning of the writing process rather than at the end. There are so many different stories out there that you are bound to have some similarities to the other stories that people are telling.

There is nothing wrong with having some similarities between your work and the work of other people, and because the human brain is trained to look for patterns, comparisons are inevitable. Just be aware of what is out there and that in general, comments will be made.

5) Know When to Quit

You of course want to know everything about the era or subject that you are writing about, but remember that that is generally impossible. There will always be things that you miss and things that no one can know.

You are going to make mistakes. This is a hard thing to hear, especially if, like many writers, you have a lot of investment in getting the story right.

Writing can lend itself to endless revisions and also to endless research as you try to be true to the story that you are trying to tell, and it is important not to let this impulse stop you from finishing anything.

When you are looking to make sure that your research is as complete as it can be, try to look at it from all sides. When you feel comfortable with the topic, it is time to move on and start your writing.

Research is the way that you give your writing authority and how you can make sure that you know what you are talking about, but do not let it get in the way of actually writing your book.

If someone calls you on something that is wrong, fix it if you can, and if it is too late, apologize and state that you will do better in the future.

6) Real Stories, Real Feelings

There are many great stories out there that are based on real life. Chances are good that your family has one, and there is a great temptation to mine that for your book. They say that everything is fair game when you are telling a great story, but don't forget that for some people, those stories strike much closer to home.

If you are going to write a novel or memoir that features or involves people who are still living, take a moment to think about what it could mean to them. What does your story say about them, and how are they going to handle it?

For example, if your memoir features incidents of abuse or abandonment, how do you feel about casting others in such a light? If your relationship with the people involved has improved and you want it to stay good, consider thinking about what this could mean.

Some people decide that some stories should simply not be told for the preservation of family peace, and some people believe that their stories are important enough that they need to be told regardless of who is involved. Both sides have valid points, and you have to decide where you want to stand.

If you are writing a story with real people involved, it is often in your best interests to talk with them about it. If your grandmother has a story where she survived poverty and hardship, she might feel that those stories are better off forgotten. This is something that you want to respect.

Also remember that some people get very angry when their actions are discussed in anything resembling a public form. Keep your own safety in mind as well.

Writing things based on real people is always tricky, but you will find that it can be rewarding as well. When you are writing something that talks about people you care about, do not leave them in the dark. Be willing to share your work, to be corrected, and to be as true to the material as you can be.

7) Research vs. Story

Once you have done a lot of research on a certain topic, you want to put it in your story. You have all of this interesting information, and of course you want to use it.

However, before you do so, make sure that you stop and consider whether that information actually belongs in the story. If you did a lot of research into how to make clothes from the Elizabethan era, you may want to talk all about the corsets, the seaming, the underwear and the headpieces.

However, the thing to remember is that your research is meant to provide you with a great backdrop to the story, and it is meant to keep you from making serious errors along the way. It is not meant to take center stage in the way that it would if you were a historian who was writing a non-fiction book!

Your novel needs to make sure that you are striking the right balance between telling people about the era or activity in question and overwhelming them with information.

When in doubt, ask what a bit of information adds to the scene and whether the reader needs to know it. For example, a reader might need to know that Victorian clothing was fastened up the back so that well-born ladies could not dress themselves. The reader does not need to know about the fact that the corset was made of whalebone and about how the corsetry industry was closely connected to the whaling industry at the time.

It can be pretty heart-breaking when you do hours of research and have plenty of notes only to realize that you have done it all for two lines in the text that no one will ever notice. This can be rough, but you need to go ahead with the story.

The important thing is that you know the information, and that you have added to the reality of the scene. All knowledge is useful, and you can always use the research again on a later project.

8) Write It Down

When you are in the middle of some very exciting research and you are very excited about your story, it can be a little tough to remember to write things down. You think that a fact is so cool and so interesting that of course you will remember it, but unfortunately, the human mind does not work that way!

If you run across a piece of information that you know you want to keep, or even if you have a piece of information that is vaguely interesting, take a moment to write it down. This is something that will be very good for you later.

Some people have great memories and do not need to write things down, but that is far from true for everyone.

There are a lot of ways to take notes, but if you are someone who loves to write things down with a pen or pencil, consider using note cards. As you are writing your novel, write down all of the facts that will go into it.

Even if you feel it is a little wasteful, write down one fact per note card. If you have different facts for different areas of study, make sure that you color-code them. The bigger your work is, the better off you are going to be if you have note cards for when you need to find a specific piece of information.

If you are someone who takes better notes when they are on the computer, keep a few files dedicated to your research in a folder. You may think that you will always know where you have put something, but the more you write, the more your folders will simply balloon.

Create a different research folder for every single topic, and be willing to pop in everything that you think you will need, whether you are looking at images, maps, or bookmarks. This folder will come in handy as you are looking around for more information.

9) Save Your Research

There is nothing more frustrating than doing hours and hours of research and then realizing that you are not going to be using that particular research at all. Things happen, stories change, and suddenly you no longer need to know what it was like to drive a Russian tank in World War II.

It is disappointing, but do not delete your research out of frustration. The research that you do today might help you tomorrow, and once the information has percolated in your brain for a while, you never know what is going to pop up.

There is no such thing as wasted information, so take a moment to save the files and to add to them from time to time as you find more things.

Writers are often depositories of odd information and experts on the strange. This gives them a more rounded worldview, and it really does help them figure out how to write better.

When you go to do your writing, always remember to learn as much as you can. You never know when it will come in handy!

Chapter 5) Writing Day to Day

After all of that prep work, you may already feel as if you have run a marathon, but the real work has only just begun. Simply having the research and the planning materials in front of you is essential, but now you need to get down to doing the grunt work of simply putting words on the page.

For some people, this is harder than others, and one thing that you need to remember is that everyone has a method that works for them. If a method that has worked before seems to be failing you at the moment, try another. Just because something let you write five thousand good words in one day doesn't mean that it will help you do the same thing the day after that.

These are tips that you can use in any order you wish. Remember that after the structure is set and the research is done, the name of the game is getting your butt in the chair and the words on the page.

What can you do to make sure that you are getting the kind of word count that you need to finish your story? Try some of these techniques and keep trying different things until you find something that really does work for you.

1) Set Some Time To Write

As human beings, we respond best to patterns, and setting habits for your writing is a great thing to do for yourself. You should set some time aside to write every day, but there is no rule about when to do it and how much to do.

The truth is that this is something that is different for every single person, and the only person who can answer what is right for you is you!

For example, if you are someone who works best when you first get up, consider doing your writing first thing in the morning. If you are a night owl who works best when everyone is asleep, do it then.

Remember that your work does not have to happen all at once. Some people state that they work best in long and uninterrupted chunks, but other people prefer to break their writing up into 20-minute intervals.

2) How Much Should I Write Every Day?

The question of how much you should write every day is a personal one. Some famous writers churn out thousands of words every day, though it varies from person to person how many of those words get edited out.

Other people write very few words every day, trying to make every word that they put down count. There is nothing wrong with this approach either.

Some people are very excited by National Novel Writing Month, where they join with many others to try to write a 40,000 word novel in a month. This event requires around 1600 words written per day, which many people find challenging.

At the end of the day, it is up to you. Just remember that it is always better to have words down on paper than to simply think about it, and that something is always better than nothing!

3) Switch Things Around

When you getting started with your writing, or even when you have been writing for a while, be aware of how you feel. Sometimes a routine that felt great at the beginning starts to feel more like a strait jacket.

When you start feeling like you are chained to your chair, the truth is that you are thinking more about how trapped you are feeling than how well your writing is going.

Be willing to change things up, even if it is hard. A small change of scenery can make a difference. For example, if you are used to writing at your desk, think about trying to write at the library or a coffee shop instead. Even moving from a desk to a couch can make a big difference.

The only person who decides how to work is you.

4) Warming Up

When you are an athlete, the coaches and trainers never let you do a single thing until you are warmed up. Warming up prevents you from being stiff and slow when you are actually doing things, and it works the same way for writers.

Before you sit down to work on your story, take just five or ten minutes to warm up. There are a number of interesting exercises for you to try. Check out a few below or come up with your own ideas. They just have to be short.

* Write a 100-word story. This story is called a drabble, and it is actually harder than it looks!

* List every word you can think of that begins with the letter F.

* Write about the last time you felt truly sad.

* Tell a fairy tale or myth in your own words, and once again, keep it short!

* Write a short scene with your characters as people of the opposite sex.

*Imagine how your life might look if you lived in a different era.

Short writing exercises can be a great way to get you settled for the day.

5) Fighting Writer's Block

The fear of the empty page has stopped far more people than you might ever have imagined, and if the day ever comes when you are facing an empty page with no idea what to put down, it is a terrifying thing.

However, the important thing to remember is that writer's block can be faced and it can be beaten.

If you are facing writer's block, do not back down. Do not throw your hands up and simply say that it is useless!

Instead, simply start writing any way that you can. If you are typing, switch to writing longhand. If you are working on a story, switch to a poem.

There is more than one way to get into a narrative, and writer's block is just an obstacle. It is not something that needs to take over your writing dream.

This sounds very easy to say, but the truth is that the first case of writer's block is always the hardest. Make sure that you stick with your writing and that you do not let this issue get in the way.

6) Showing Others Your Work

Writing is an interesting thing. It can be intensely personal, but it is something that is expressly created for an artist. Some writers write only for themselves, while others do not feel that their work is complete until someone else has read it.

The question often comes up of whether you should show your work to someone else before you finish it. Some people feel that this dilutes their vision, while others find that it gives them hope.

When you are wondering whether you should show someone what you are working on, the answer really relies on what you hope to get out of it and whether you can get it from the person that you are showing it to.

For example, if you need help on a plot point, show it to someone who reads the genre in which you are writing, and be ready to take any critique they can give you. It is often better to ask for this kind of help when you are stuck on a specific point. Asking for a full critique of the work before it is done can end up being painful and demoralizing.

If you just need some encouragement, say so to your reader. Anyone who knows anything about writing knows how tough it is so they can help by keeping their comments constructive and their tone encouraging. There is a place for more precise criticism, but generally, it is not while you are still in the midst of writing it.

7) Writing as a Job

Writing is a job like any other, and you will find that the more you do it, the easier it will get. However, at the beginning, it can be a little hard to get past the original thought that you are sitting down to have fun!

Let that thought stand as long as you can, but remember that there will be days where 5000 words don't just fly from your fingers. There are going to be days when you struggle to put down 500 words, or 250, or even 100 words.

If it helps you to think about writing as a job, consider mentally paying yourself for your work. Give yourself a rate per word, and write until that rate is satisfied. This is something that can make it a lot easier for you to give your progress a real world feeling.

8) Do Other Things

Writing is fueled by reading, but in many ways, it is fueled by everything in your life. Writing may be your passion and your avocation, but it does not exist in a vacuum.

For example, you may have a great story about a writer, but most people are getting pretty tired of hearing about the writer who writes about how hard it is to write and be a writer!

From time to time, take a break from your computer. Some people work for a few days straight and then spend some time away, while other people make sure that they get out for a walk to see their friends and family throughout the day. This is something that can make you feel a lot healthier and a lot more balanced.

If you actually let writing take over your life, your work is going to suffer for it.

9) Skip the Writer Stereotype

Some people are very attached to the image of the suffering writer, the depressed artist who is suffering from one or more addictions and who has to wait for the muse to appear.

As a matter of fact, writing is a job. You do not need to fulfill this image to be a writer, and you do not need to suffer to produce great art.

Skip the dramatics and get back to work.

10) Don't Wait for the Muse

If you can only write when inspiration strikes you, you are not going to be writing for a very long time. Some days, it is going to be a trudge getting from point A to point B.

Writing is as much a craft as it is an art, and when you are in a spot where you are feeling stuck, practice, experience, and sheer perseverance comes to your rescue. Take a moment to think about what needs to happen and then write it.

A lot of people cannot tell the difference between writing that felt inspired and writing that was a trudge when they look back later, and in the end, if you tell a great story, it does not matter how you got there!

11) Forgive Yourself

You are going to have days when you cannot make the goals that you have set for yourself. You may have weeks or months when you don't touch your manuscript. The important thing to remember is that there is no length of time that is too long for you to return and try again!

Some people get stalled for years, but if they want the story to exist badly enough, it will happen.

If you have let your story sit for some time, make the time to go back to it. Just because you have let it sit for ten days does not mean that you are going to let it sit for eleven, so pull it out, and get back to writing!

12) Dressing Up

Some people do just fine if they are writing in their pajamas or even when they work in their underwear. It is all about what makes you feel comfortable and productive, but dressing up to do your writing can give your body a clue that it is time to get to work.

This does not mean that you need to dress up in formal attire, but sometimes it is best to stay in regular street clothes when you do your work instead of slipping into something more comfortable.

Comfortable clothes like sweat suits and pajamas tell your body that you are done with work for the day. On the other hand, clothes that are a little more restrictive tell you that there is still work to be done.

One rule that works for writers, just like it works for anyone else who works at home, is that you should put your shoes on when you go to work. Having shoes on keeps you grounded and it gives you a little hint regarding the fact that you need to stay focused if you want to get done.

13) Taking Breaks

It might seem a little funny to hear that you need to take breaks after you have read so much about being diligent, but the truth is that working in long and uninterrupted spates can really hurt you after a while. Eyestrain and stiffness can result if you stay in one place for too long, and you will discover that taking breaks offers a much-needed relief.

Consider looking up the Pomodoro method online, which is

meant to maximize creativity. Feel free to modify it into something that works for you.

The Pomodoro method uses a timed work period followed by a short break, all moderated by a timer to tell you when to work and when to stop.

The key to this method for many people is starting it in the first place. Once you get the timer going, stick with it. Modify it as you need to, but remember that the key is to keep your work periods short enough that you are feeling energized and to take breaks throughout so that you can recharge your battery as you need to.

This is something that can help you get through a long day of writing without allowing you to feel burned out.

14) Rough Drafts Can Be Rough

A rough draft is a personal thing. The only thing that stays the same is that everyone has to do them! When you first start writing, you may be convinced that because you are being so careful, you will be able to get away with sending off your manuscript as it is.

This is a false belief. No matter what you write or how careful you are, you need to go back and look it over, and that is what a rough draft is

Some people have very careful rough drafts, and their edits end up being mostly fixes in terms of grammar and syntax. However, the people who write like this are very careful indeed!

Other people have very, very sketchy rough drafts. Their rough drafts are more like very wordy outlines and whole sections might be missing even when they consider the draft done.

Either approach is legitimate as it puts you closer to a finished product.

One of the best reasons to take advantage of a piece of writing being a rough draft is that it takes some of the pressure off of you. Not everything needs to be done right this moment, and you will discover that there is a great deal of freedom that can come from saying that you are skipping a difficult scene and moving forward.

For example, if you know that a fight scene needs to happen, but you are not sure how you want to handle it, insert a note that says "FIGHT SCENE HERE" and just move on. Perhaps you will pick up the fight scene in the next session, or maybe you will pick it up much later.

This is a technique that is used by many writers. For example, George R. R. Martin, who wrote the series, *A Song of Ice and Fire*, wrote most of the book before returning to the infamous scene that is known as the Red Wedding. He found that the events of the scene were so intense and heartbreaking that he put off writing it until he was nearly done.

Something that needs to be remembered if you consider using this method is that you should know what happens in the scene. You should have a clear idea of what is going to go into the scene. This makes it much safer for you to skip it.

If the scene is unclear in your mind, like there is a dialogue between two characters and you are not quite sure how it is going to play out, do not skip it. Figure out what is going to happen, and then move forward. Skipping things that you are unsure about can make later writing unusable.

Your rough draft can be as rough as you need it to be. No one will see it except you and the people that you choose to show it to.

Think of it as the scaffolding that is used to support theater sets. It is very important, but it is not something that people will see.

15) Revision as You Write?

If you are a writer, you must be aware of the fact that there is a certain amount of control that you love to have. People who become writers love to have control over their projects, and although this can be a very good thing in some respects, it can actually hurt you in others.

As you write, you are going to make mistakes. Maybe you realize that the thing that you wrote yesterday does not jibe with something that you have decided about the way that the story is going to go. Maybe you realize that you have a better idea for a certain scene.

You may be tempted to go back and fix it, and if it is a relatively minor thing, you should do so. However, if it is a large thing or if you realize that you keep going back to fix things rather than progressing steadily, it is likely a better idea for you to simply go back and to treat things like that in edits.

Editing as you go is a possibility for some people, but for other people, it prevents them from actually progressing.

16) Getting Away From It All

Writer's block can be beaten, but burnout is another thing entirely. When you have been focused on writing for the last several weeks or months, you may quickly realize that you are getting tired of it. If you heave a sigh every time you sit down at your keyboard, and if you get a little angry when you have to write, it is time to start paying closer attention.

You might be suffering from burnout, and it is something that happens no matter how much you love writing. Burnout is a rough thing to deal with, and if you are not careful, it can delay a project for months or even years!

Basically, when you do something too often, even when it is something that you know you love, you are courting burnout. This condition occurs because there are many parts to every human being. You are a writer, but you also have family members, friends, hobbies and other things that you enjoy.

Writing can be a rather insidious hobby due to the fact that it is something that can be done nearly anywhere and whenever you want to do it. This means that you can slide it into all sorts of times and spaces, and after a while, it can be hard to get away from it. Writing can be an addictive behavior just like everything else!

If you are worried that you are suffering from burnout, take a step back and consider what kind of space your story has taken in your life. If you have a tough time remembering when you were doing anything besides writing, you may be suffering from burnout.

The answer is to take a break before your mind and body decide that you need one regardless of what else you are doing. People who burn out have to spend significant amounts of time recovering, so watch out for this.

Chapter 6) Joining a Writing Group

One of the tools that you can use when you want to write your story is to surround yourself with writers. When you have other writers around you, you will find yourself thinking about the action of writing more often, you have "co-workers" who can sympathize with you regarding where you are at, and you can share some of the victories and some of the downsides with people who know where you are coming from.

How can you get the most out of a writer's group?

1) Finding Your Writing Group

There are several ways to find a writing group that works for you. If at all possible, take the time to look locally. If you have transportation, see what you can do about getting out to meet people. If you have been doing nothing but working and writing, taking the time out to actually go out and to see people can make a big difference to your mood.

Sites like Meetup.org are a good place to start, but you should also check the bulletin boards at your local libraries and coffee shops. If you go to school or if you work at one, you may find a campus-centered writing group that can help you.

Do not underestimate the appeal of online writing groups either. There are enough writing groups online that it is very easy to get a little overwhelmed, but if you are wiling to take a little bit of time and energy to sort things out, you are going to be able to find people who can help you.

Look for people who are writing on about the same level as you are and who are writing something similar in the same genre. If you are a speculative fiction writer, you want to talk with people who also work in that genre. While someone who writes romance will have plenty to offer you with regards to plot pacing, dialogue and structure, they do not have the same genre conventions as you do.

2) Writing Group Size

When it comes to picking a writing group, the general consensus is that the smaller the group is, the better off you will be. While a group of three or four people is on the small side, nine or ten members is getting a little unwieldy.

The key is to make sure that your writing group allows you to be helped while also being helpful to others. With too many people, there will simply be too many people who all need to make themselves heard.

3) Assessing Attitude

Writing groups are just like any other group of people. Some work very well, some have great intentions but never get off the ground, and others are simply toxic. Writing groups can give some very destructive personalities a place to get their aggressions out on other people, so be wary of this.

When you first visit an already-established writer's group, consider taking the first night just to sit and observe. Do the members of the writing group treat each other with respect? Do they listen without interrupting, and do they have a genuine urge to improve each other's writing?

If you notice that there are some members who seem too afraid to speak, or if you notice that there are a lot of casual and not-so-casual put-downs being used, it is time to leave.

Never believe anyone who says that writers have to toughen up. While taking good critique is one thing, taking insults is another. You never have to stand there and take another person's insults or abuse, and if you have a gut feeling that this is what is happening, just leave.

People actually do better when they are encouraged and when they are shown how to improve instead of simply being told how they have fallen short.

Writing groups are great places to hone your craft, but if the only thing that you are learning is that you can take increasingly greater and more intense forms of abuse, there are definitely better places for you to be spending your time.

4) Critiquing Others

One reason to join a writing group is to learn how writing works. Your process is not the only one out there, and there are many other tips and tricks that you can learn along the way. When you see how others write, you will quickly see what you might do differently and how you might be able to proceed.

When you join a writing group, you will be expected to give critique as well as take it. If you have never critiqued work before, this can be a little tough.

Start simply by reading the work that you have been handed. Read it as you would any causal story or piece of writing that you would pick up in a magazine or on a blog. Note your reactions as you go along, but do not stop to pick them apart.

Then read through a second time, going slower, and making sure that you are looking for things like discrepancies in the logic, for grammar and syntax errors, and for issues with description and word choice.

Finally, make a third pass through the work, looking for anything you missed, and write down your overall impressions of the work. This is something that can make a huge difference to the effect of your critique.

When you go to present your critiques, be polite but firm. Never insult someone else's writing, but be honest about how you felt. Encompassing statements like "I hated this," or "I loved this!" are not helpful at all.

Instead, make comments like, "this section made me extremely uncomfortable due to these factors," "I enjoyed this particular part," and "this section is weaker and does not make much sense when compared to this section."

Part of being in a good critique group is making sure that you contribute as well, and when you do this, you will find that your own writing improves on top of it all.

5) Assessing Your Writing Group

A writing group needs to serve a purpose. There is nothing wrong with going out with a group and having coffee or a good meal while chatting about your lives, but this will not necessarily make you a better writer. Writing groups do best when they stay centered on the work at hand. If people are simply too caught up in being social, the group will not work, and it will end up simply being a fairly pleasant social hour rather than something that can help you to achieve your writing goals.

If you are concerned that the group is oriented a little too much towards the social arena, try to steer things towards work. If you have too much trouble with this, simply find another group!

6) Starting Your Own Writing Group

They say that when you want to do something right, you have to do it yourself, and one area where that may be true for you is in finding your writing group.

If you cannot find a group that really works for you, it might be in your best interests to look for a group of people that you yourself can bring together. This is something that can take up a lot of time, but you can also help yourself while helping others at the same time.

Some people choose to start with people that they know who write, and other people choose to start with strangers. Think about whom you want in your group and choose accordingly. Decide if the group is going to be open to anyone who drops in or if there is going to be any sort of requirement for people to gain admittance.

Some groups request that people submit a piece of work before they can gain admittance to the group, while other people simply say that everyone is welcome. For your own sake and your own sanity, it might be best for you to simply put a limit on who is allowed in and how many people you want to deal with.

When you are deciding how things should be set up, remember that it is usually best to have people read the work before they show up. Writing is distributed one session and then reviewed during another. This is a good way to make sure that no one has to sit awkwardly while people around them are reading their material.

7) Understand How You Work With Groups

Some people work well with others, and other people definitely prefer a more solitary way to work towards the completion of their novel. If you are someone who prefers to be alone, and if the idea of working with others is seriously something that alarms you, do not force yourself to seek others out.

If you can handle it, consider joining a writing group online and making introductions there. If you do not want to join a writing group at all, you do not have to.

It is a good idea to get other eyes on your work, but it is not vital. You can progress on your own, but you should understand that this is a tool that you are choosing not to use.

Think about what you want out of your experience with a writing group, but do not force yourself. You may realize that you want something that is very different from what is being offered. You may find yourself in a group of people who discuss writing in a way that does not feel right to you, and you might find that their attitude simply does not work with your story or the way you do things.

Remember that the biggest reason to be in a writing group is to improve your writing. Unless your writing is being improved, there is no reason to stay unless you simply enjoy the company.

If you are having a rough time with the group, you do not need permission to quit. Take a moment to consider what you need, and to think whether your specific group or any group at all will help you.

There are many, many different ways to be a successful writer, so do not think that you have to follow a single group's rules or that you need a group at all.

If you are someone who works best when they are independent, there is nothing wrong with that at all.

8) Do Your Homework

One of the problems with joining a writing group is that it is a lot like doing schoolwork without having the pressure of failing.

The truth is that we are all busy. We all have lives to get to, and writing is something that is important to us, but maybe the writing of others is a lot less important than our own.

If you are going to join a writing group, always be very clear about what you are going to do and how you are going to help other people. There are people who think that a writing group is all about them, but these people cause problems.

When you are giving work to review, give that review as much effort as you hope others would give to yours. Be diligent about marking and offering your best critiques, and do not just join in with the conversation when it has something to do with your work.

The thing that makes a writer's group work is good will, and it is all about finding ways to help everyone improve at least a little.

A writing group is a commitment, so once you sign on, make sure that you keep up as best you can. There will be people there who do not write in a way that is fun for you. There may be people there who write things that you would consider offensive.

Think about what you are willing to do for others, and though you should always set limits, be willing to give them your best efforts.

9) Saying Rough Things

Let's face it, not all writers are created equal. Some are better than others, some are just getting started, and still others need to start from the ground up when it comes to writing.

The longer you spend in writing groups, the sooner you are going to run into someone who has some real problems with the way that they write, whether they cannot put together a sentence or that their plots are just recycled from television.

People like this have it tough, and they do not need you to make it tougher. However, they are also not going to get better unless someone shows them how to write, and you can help there.

Never say that their writing is terrible. That is both unkind and unhelpful! Instead, be as blunt and kind as you can. If you can tell that something is not working, point it out to them. Show them things that they can work on and how they can improve.

Remember that you do not need to offer a fix for everything. Sometimes, it is enough for an editor to know that something is wrong, and they do not necessarily need to know how to fix it.

You will come across people who are terrible, but remember that even if they will never be great, they can get better. Be kind and sympathetic, and do your best to be encouraging.

It does not take much to make someone's day, so be willing to talk to him or her about his or her work. Do not lie, do not say that it is better than it is, but remember that there is good that can be found and built upon. Sometimes, the person in question is not a romance writer, but they might make a great non-fiction article writer!

10) Being Okay With Being Alone

If you want to write, you should resign yourself to being alone for large amounts of it. If you are a real social butterfly, this can be something that really does seem strange or uncomfortable to you, but the truth is that writing, at the most basic level, is you alone with your computer.

If you are someone who is used to having lots of people around, take it slow. Write on your own for short periods of time. A writing group can help you stay on top of things while satisfying your need for company, but just remember that you should always be willing to work on this solitary pursuit.

11) Do I Need a Writing Partner?

If you have a friend or loved one who also writes, it can be tempting to see if you can form a writing partnership. There are absolutely people who make writing partnerships work, but you have to think carefully before you decide if you are one of them.

In a writing partnership, you must relinquish part of your control over a manuscript. This is something that can be very hard, particularly if you are looking at a manuscript that you have considered to be yours for years and years. The truth of the matter is that when you engage with someone as a writing partner, you are bringing on their strengths and their weaknesses.

Before you even start plotting with someone, think about how you can divide up the duties. Are you someone who loves to write dialogue but hates writing actions scenes? Can you create plots but hate filling them out?

A great writing partner is someone who steps in for you when you get to things that you have a difficulty doing on your own. They compensate for your weak points and you do the same for them. It is a partnership, and you will find that if you can form a partnership with the right person, it can be an engaging one. Take a moment to think about who you know who can help you make your book better.

Do not engage in a writing partnership with someone just because you like them or because you think they are a good friend. Writing together is like working together, and it means that you trust them to do what they say they will.

When you find someone whose style matches your own, whose goals are similar to yours, and who you can work with on a day to day basis, you have found someone who might be a good writing partner. This is the bare minimum!

Chapter 7) Revisions

When you finish your novel, you may feel as though you have climbed a mountain. You have gotten to the top after a treacherous journey, and you can be proud of where you have been and what you have done.

Revising, then, is like realizing that the mountain is actually a lot taller than you thought!

If you are a writer, you need to revise your writing. No one really writes perfect rough drafts. No one actually produces work that is publishable or even ready for submissions when they first finish it.

What can you do to start the round of revisions, and how can you make sure that you catch all the errors that you made?

1) Put It Away

Writing a story that you care about is an intense experience. It can take you to places inside yourself that you never knew existed, and it can leave you feeling exhilarated or despairing, depending on the moment.

Just like any other intense emotion, however, it is not recommended that you make big decisions while you are feeling this fraught!

When you have finished your manuscript, back it up, and then put it away. Back away from the writing and the work, and simply let it sit.

Depending on how you feel about it and how tired you are, you might let it sit for a few weeks to a few months. Basically, the more time you have away from it, the easier it will be to come back with fresh eyes.

The more time you have away from your work, the more objective you can be when you come back.

2) Read as a Reader

When you are coming back go your manuscript, you are going to be able to look at it with fresh eyes. Take advantage of this and simply sit back and read it as a reader would.

For your very first read-through, resist the urge to make any changes. As a matter of fact, you can simply open it as a read only file or a PDF, which does not allow you to make changes. This is difficult, because no matter how careful you are, you will see problems, but this is a unique opportunity.

After you finish it and before you edit it, you will be able to see the novel as someone else does. You'll be able to see the flaws that hurt it and the great things about it as well. This is something that will become more and more difficult as time goes on.

Sit back, pour yourself a hot cup of tea or coffee and start reading. Read your novel as if you were an outsider with an interest in the topic being discussed, and simply collect your first impressions.

Be as honest as you can, and as you read, keep some notes by your side. Do not bother making grammatical edits or syntax errors, but just make a general count of things that you like and things that you don't like.

It might feel a little vain, but remember that you are allowed to be proud of yourself. You have created a full story that has never existed in the world before. You have told a story that cannot be told by anyone except you.

Embrace and revel in it before editing and revising make you tired and irritated with yourself.

3) Print and Mark

It is simple to leave the manuscript on the computer and to correct it there, but there is something both satisfying and more efficient about printing out the manuscript and going over it with a pen.

When you have a physical document in front of you, it encourages you to look at it in a new way. You are using a pen to make changes, and you can be more ruthless about it, crossing out things that you might have been less brave about if you were on the computer.

4) Limit Yourself

Editing, whether you are doing it for yourself or someone else, is hard work. It is tiring, is it very detail-oriented, and it is frustrating.

When you want to make sure that you can get through the entire manuscript without getting angry or upset, limit yourself to a certain number of pages per day.

Start by editing ten or twenty pages a day, and then if you can take more, upgrade your rate accordingly.

Remember that writing and editing are two sides of the same coin. You cannot do one without the other, and some people will find that one half takes up a lot more space than the other half.

5) Bring In Friends

If you are in a position where you are looking at a piece of writing that you have created and you think that you cannot look at it any more, it is time to bring in some friends. A good friend helps you move bodies, but a great friend will sit with you and go through your writing exhaustively, helping you sort out what you need to sort out.

Some people bring in their friends throughout the process, asking them to check on things as they go and to consider plot structure and execution. Other people do not show their friends their work until it is complete, allowing them to see the work as a whole.

Either approach is fine, so just settle on the one that suits you. Editing is work. If you have ever edited your own work or someone else's, you will realize this very quickly. You are asking your friends to do you a favor, so remember that they may not have the time or the inclination.

Ask them to mark up a physical manuscript or to track changes on a document if they are so inclined. This is a fairly close editing pass, and if they are willing to do it for you, thank them profusely!

They may be more comfortable simply talking with you over dinner or coffee regarding your manuscript. The more eyes that you have on your text the better, so simply let them give you feedback in whatever way makes you the most comfortable.

Remember that you are not compelled to take anyone's advice. Sometimes, you and your friends might disagree on what is going on with the work. They may feel that you need to take something out while you have good reasons to keep it in.

You are the final authority on the matter, but you will also find that their opinion should mean something. Always thank them for the time that they took to read your work.

6) Keep Editing

You will never be more aware of the faults of your work than when you are editing. Suddenly you will be able to see every shortcut that you took and every way in which you do not compare to your favorite authors.

It is very easy to get discouraged while you are editing. You may feel that the issues are bad enough that you do not want to bother fixing them. Suddenly, it might seem easier for you to tear it all down and to start over from scratch.

Resist the urge to destroy your work and start over from scratch. There are no perfect novels, and your work is only going to get better from being edited. The important thing is that you have something to edit.

Sometimes, editing is a difficult thing. It takes time and effort, and sometimes you just do not want to do it. Unless you are on a tight deadline, take a break. Nothing bad is going to happen if you edit ten pages one day and just three the next. As long as things are moving forwards, you will be fine.

Frustration is normal and acceptable, and breaks are important when you are doing something that is so important to you.

7) Accepting Editing Help Gracefully

We covered some of this material in the chapter about writing groups, but there is some information that should be brought up here.

Someone who edits your work is doing you a favor, especially if they are not being paid to do so. You do not need to take their advice, but you should always listen to it.

Do not try to argue them out of their opinion. If they say something that strikes you as false, remember to let them get through the entire thought. Do not interrupt them or correct them. You never know when they might reason something out for themselves or when they might have an addition that will make things make a lot more sense!

When you are talking to someone about your work, do not criticize their critique, but also remember that you should not allow them to be rude to you. If they are insulting or otherwise not helpful, simply end the conversation.

Dealing with editors is a tough thing for most writers. You have put a lot of time, effort, and love into something that is designed for an audience, and there is a good chance that you are quite invested in it!

Then you hand it over to someone who is specifically looking for flaws. Granted, they are looking for flaws in order to make it better, but this is not necessarily a comfort when you are feeling sensitive about it.

Just remember that if you are feeling a little nervous or angry about an edit, give yourself time to cool off. Some people do not read the edits on their manuscript for quite some time in order to get themselves used to the idea.

Above all, always remember to be polite and to be appreciative of the fact that they took the time to edit it. At the very least, this is good practice for professional editing somewhere down the line.

8) Learning to Ask Questions

If you are someone who is deeply invested in getting the most out of your editing, take a moment to think about what you need.

If you hand someone a manuscript, there is a good chance that they will read it, and then when you speak with them again, they will shrug, bewildered, when you ask them what they thought of it. They'll tell you that it is good and that they liked it, but in the grand scheme of things, this is less handy than you might wish.

When you hand your manuscript over, ask them to read with a few things in mind. Ask them specific questions, and if they are willing, ask them to look for specific issues.

For example, instead of just handing your manuscript over, make sure that you are handing it over while saying things like "I'm curious as to what you think about the dialog," or "could you watch out for issues where I am rushing? I am afraid I might have an issue with that."

This is a good way to get a very directed idea of what your editors think. Remember that they were not trained to do this, but that an untrained eye can respond to you as a reader would.

9) When Am I Done?

The best thing about writing a story is that eventually you will get to the end. The worst thing about editing is that you could honestly do it forever! Editing is a refining process, and as we have discussed before, there is no such thing as a perfect manuscript. At best, you are going to have a manuscript that makes you feel proud and that others will enjoy reading.

No matter how often you go over it, there will be mistakes that you miss. No matter how carefully you research, you are going to

74

get things wrong. This is part of writing, and in many cases, it is part of being human.

At some point, you will simply have to say that the manuscript is as complete as you can make it, and call it good. Do what you can, but when you are simply going over it to nitpick small details, it is as complete as you can make it.

10) Set Goals

When you are editing, remember that you should always know what you are looking for. You will be reading the document several times, and ideally, you will always be catching mistakes and problems as you go.

For example, when you read it for the first time, pay special attention to the dialog and the way that people talk. The next time you read it, make sure that you consider the structure of the story and your ability to keep everything on track.

Editing is essentially your way of making your story more presentable to the people who want to buy it. It means that you need to pay attention to every kind of mistake that you can make with a manuscript, and that you also need to consider what it means when you are thinking about how to make it better.

Do not reduce your editing to simply reading the manuscript. While simply reading the manuscript as you would normally proceed with reading a book is a good place to start, you need to be a critical reader.

Sit down and set goals for yourself as you look into how you are going to be doing your editing. What are your goals when you sit down? How many pages are you going to be getting through, and how can you make sure that you reach your goals?

Remember that the more willing you are to break your work into chunks, the fresher your eyes will be. Studies show that we are the most perceptive at the beginning and at the end of a project. That is why short study and editing sessions, which give you more beginnings and endings to work with, can make such a difference when it comes to improving your editing.

When you want to make sure that you are doing a good job with your editing, remember that you need to ask yourself specific questions and to set plenty of goals.

11) Fact Checking

One important thing that you can do when you are looking at revising your novel is fact checking. In this process, you figure out if everything that you put down is in fact true. This is especially important if you are looking at work that pertains to a period of history within the last fifty years or so, as it will be very easy for people to prove you wrong if you happen to have made a mistake.

Start with the simple things that you need to verify. If you are writing about battles from the Civil War, for example, take a moment to think about checking the dates, the generals that were present and the things that you have portrayed.

The truth is that between reading the information, taking the notes and writing the story, things can get quite mangled. It is a lot like playing a game of Telephone, where the facts get increasingly distorted.

Sit down and skim your manuscript, circling any spots where you think some doubt or uncertainty might have set in. As you go, read with a fresh mind, and be open to doubt. If something suddenly seems a little implausible to you, there is a good chance that it might seem a little implausible to someone else as well!

12) Reward Yourself

Finishing your manuscript is something that looks very impressive, and as you do so, you have a big file with an entire novel in it as a reward.

When you finish editing, you just have the same manuscript, but now you are tired of it, you can see nothing but errors and you are convinced that nothing good will ever come of it.

Remember that finishing your novel edits is just as important as finishing the raw word count as well, and you need and deserve a celebration.

Take the night off and go and celebrate with your friends, or simply take a moment to breathe and to treat yourself to pizza and a movie. Editing is not fun, and it can leave you feeling very tired and distressed.

The good news is that the editing is over. The bad news is that now you need to start submitting it!

Chapter 8) Conventional Publishing

If you pick up any guide on publishing, you will find that it assumes that you are going to be going down the conventional publishing route. Conventional publishing was the only game in town for decades, but as of this point in time, it is actually one of three options.

With the internet taking over everybody's life and the vast majority of people order books via the internet, it has become less important to have your book shown on the shelves of physical book stores. Lots of book stores are suffering because people hang out on the internet and no longer in book stores. Therefore, online is where you need to be. Everything you need to know about self publishing your book online is explained in www.worldwideselfpublishing.com. It is the best self publishing product I have come across. It tells you absolutely everything you need to know if you want to self publishing your book. **Surprisingly, for £41 or $67, you can publish your hard copy book and have it distributed all over the world, including listing on all the Amazon sites! Unbelievable but true.**

This is possible with POD, Print on Demand, which had an absolutely huge effect on the book publishing industry. All is explained in www.worldwideselfpublishing.com

More about self publishing later in this book.

What do you need to know about conventional publishing, and how can it affect you?

1) How Does It Work?

When you go to see professional conventional publishers, you choose a publisher that might be interested in your work, and then you will read their submission guidelines with extreme care. Some standard publishers still only accept paper submissions, while others have email submission standards.

You will send your work in, along with any documentation that they require, and generally, because they do not allow you to submit your work to another publisher while they have it, you wait and write something else.

If they accept your work, they will offer you a contract, which tells you how you will be paid. Most major publishing houses will offer you an advance, that is, money that is given to you against the money that they believe the book will make.

It is worth pointing out that most advances do not pay out. You do not need to return the money if this is the case; the advance represents the chance that the publisher is taking on you.

Depending on the publishing house, especially if you look into smaller presses or online presses, you may not receive an advance at all, but instead will receive a certain percentage of your sales.

Your contract will delineate what rights you are selling, and it will tell you when you should expect payments. Always read your contract carefully as it will tell you all about what you can or cannot do with your work after it has been committed to a publisher.

2) Who Should I Send My Work To?

The question of what publisher you want to submit to is a personal one. When you are looking at getting started with publications in the conventional field, there is no reason not to start at the top. Always be willing to look over the requirements, however, as each one will have different rules. Some will not allow you to make multiple submissions, and some top publishing houses do not take submissions that are not presented by an agent.

Publications like *The Writer's Market*, and sites like Duotrope.com can help you find the markets that you require. They help you figure out who is looking for work and what other people say about the publications.

Remember that you should always look up a publication's reputation before you submit to them. When you Google them, are you finding people who are angry about not being paid or people who have been abused by unfair policies? Learn from the people who have already had problems and make sure that you do not make the same mistakes.

3) Formatting

All publishers will tell you how you how they want to see your manuscript. Most of them still use the standard manuscript formatting, which is widely available on the Internet, or they might have a house style that you should adhere to.

Regardless of what kind of formatting they ask for, consider learning how to use page styles. Page styles allow you to create formats that are then used to address the formatting needs of a particular publisher. You can adjust the page styles, and through them, adjust the look of the entire manuscript.

Many people grew up formatting everything by hand, but this can cause problems when people are using different versions of different programs.

Learning to use good formatting and how page styles can work for you can relieve you of a lot of headaches later on down the line. Be willing to consider how you can save time by investing in this knowledge.

Remember that you should always check things before you send them off. Sometimes, formatting changes do odd things to manuscripts, and it is always better to find the problems and to fix them. Otherwise, you risk sending an unreadable manuscript to the people you most want to impress.

4) Double Check Everything

When you think you have everything ready for submission, put it aside for a day or two and simply stop thinking about it. Then, go back through and go down the list of things that are necessary for submission one more time.

More and more publishers are asking for things like synopses and author information, and leaving something like that out can mean months of delay if not an outright rejection. Remember that every major publisher and most of the small presses as well are simply swamped with submissions. Do not give them an excuse to dismiss your manuscript!

5) Writing a Synopsis

Many publishers require that you send along a synopsis, which they will look at before they start looking at your work. The synopsis is an important part of your submission, and if you have never written one before, it can be a little intimidating.

Basically, a synopsis describes your story by stripping it down to the main events and creating an easy tool for the publisher to preview your work. Remember that your synopsis should be as well written, clear and concise as the rest of your story. It should not be something that you throw together at the last moment.

Instead, sit down, and look over your story. Break it down to the main events and to what is going on. In many ways, you are creating a detailed outline for your story, only you are working in reverse.

Write in complete sentences and obey the requirements of the publishers. Some want synopses that are three or four pages long, and others want synopses that are much shorter.

Do not worry if breaking a story down makes your novel sound silly or dumb. The key is that you are dealing with professionals who know what they are looking for. Abbreviation makes everyone's stories sound silly, so relax!

6) Playing the Waiting Game

Technically, when you have sent off your novel, everything is over with for quite some time. All you can do is to sit down and wait out whatever time frame the publication has for responses.

In theory this is simple, but in practice, it can drive a strong person to tears. There is simply nothing to be done about the waiting; it is part and parcel of a writer's life.

If you find that you are getting antsy while waiting for a publisher's response, you might as well go back and do more writing.

However, one thing that you should consider when you are looking at making sure that you spend your time constructively is when you are due a response. No publisher is going to leave you hanging indefinitely, even if their response time stretches to nine months to a year!

Make sure that you know when you can expect a response, and consider contacting them when that time is up. A polite email can help you figure out whether your work is still being considered or how things are working with it.

Overall, do not let your writing stall while you wait. It takes time and effort to be a writer. Do not allow yourself to rest easy while you are waiting for a response. In the most optimistic scenario, they are going to love your work and ask to see if you have anything else!

Remember that the time during which you are waiting for a response is time that can easily be spent learning more and doing even more research and preparation for your next writing project.

7) Dealing With Rejection

While there are people who get accepted to a conventional publishing house with their first manuscript, the chances of this happening are diminishingly small. Rejection is a big part of a writer's life, and no matter how good your writing is, you will be dealing with rejection. This is simply the way it goes, and no one really gets every single manuscript accepted all the time.

When you get your first rejection, allow yourself to feel disappointed for a moment, but remember that it is essential for you to pick yourself back up and to submit again. Plenty of famous writers had rejection after rejection before a publishing house took a chance on them, so be persistent.

You do not have to like rejection, but like any job, writing has its downsides and rejection is one of them. Never respond angrily to a rejection, and never go on a public rant about the unfairness of your rejection. Editors and publishers are on the Internet just like you are, and while they may not remember a pitch, they will certain remember being the target of rage!

No one likes being rejected, but the truth is that it happens to everyone. If the editors had the courtesy to tell you what felt wrong or off about your piece, be very grateful.

Form rejections are a necessity for publishers who have to deal with large amounts of volume. Do not be angry if you get one. Just consider it a good thing if you do not!

8) Do I Need an Agent?

When it comes to getting published, the short answer to "do I need an agent?" is no. It is entirely possible to write a piece of fiction or non-fiction, sell it to a publishing house and become a professional writer without an agent.

However, while this is all very possible, it is still a lot easier with an agent to watch your back! An agent is the person who submits your work for you. They will take a work that you have finished or pitched, and they will bring it around to various publishing firms to see who is interested. In the event that more than one publishing house wants your work, they will evaluate the bids and help you decide whom to choose.

On top of that, your agent is also the person who will look over your contracts and help you decide as to whether they are right for you or not. A good agent will keep you informed of everything, and they will also help you figure out what is best for your career.

As you may have guessed from this long list of duties, a good agent can help you out immeasurably. They also function as a type of gatekeeper when it comes to the work that you are doing. Many agents have relationships with a wide variety of publishing houses, and because of that, they can get your manuscripts to the people who might want to buy them.

There are several publishing houses out there that do not accept manuscripts unless it is from agents. These publishing houses tend to the most exclusive ones out there, and it can be difficult to get their time otherwise.

When you decide that you want to try to find an agent, remember that not all agents handle the same thing. Some of them work with very specific publishers, and others work with very specific genres.

Remember that the preparation for finding an agent is quite close to the kind of preparation that it takes to submit your book in the first place, but if you can get your book placed with the right professional, you can find doors opening up for you.

When you are looking for an agent, do not just hit Google. Any agent that needs to advertise for their services or that is actively looking for new clients should be regarded with suspicion. There are several scams out there that are designed to target writers, and people who pretend to be agents are just one of them.

Most professional agents at this point have websites, and you should judge their websites as you would judge any other for professional content and trustworthiness.

Once you have a list of names, start searching for the names themselves. You will quickly find out whom they have worked with and what other people think of them. A good agent is someone who has good clients and who has worked with agencies that you have heard of.

Another important factor is to check whether the agent belongs to the Association of Authors Representatives. This means that they have maintained a minimum number of sales to recognized publishing houses. However, it is also worth considering that there are some agencies represented on the AAR list that have had complaints filed against them. This means that although they do make sales, they might be more interested in making money off of their clients.

Remember that good research will save you from a lot of pitfalls. If you have an idea that an agent or agency is simply too good to be true, in general, they are!

One thing that you must remember is that authors should never need to pay their agents. An agent's fees come out of the money that they take from the publisher. Some scams suggested that an agent required a reading fee before a manuscript could be considered. This is a sure sign that you are dealing with a scammer, not a real professional.

Be very wary if an agent wants you to spend any money on the publishing process, even if they do not take the money themselves. For example, one scam involved a photographer flying out to take the author's head shots, and while they never paid the agent anything, they paid the photographer.

Be very wary of anyone who asks you to spend money in order to make money, especially if they have not been able to show you any concrete results!

9) Publishers Talk

One of the things that you have to understand when it comes to the publishing agencies out there is that publishers talk. The field is a lot smaller than you realize, and when you think about it, there are plenty of conventions and other events where they will speak with one another. This is something that can work in your favor, because if your work is good and memorable but not a good fit, the publisher who has seen it might mention it to someone else.

On the other hand, if you behave badly or if you get a reputation for being someone who is difficult to work with, remember that publishers do talk, and they can spread a lot of news about you.

When you are dealing with anyone professionally, be willing to take a moment to check yourself. Are you being polite? Are you asking for something that is considered odd or special? Are you aware of where their job begins and ends and what they do every day?

If you have had a manuscript rejected, you may find that you are hurt or angry. Remember that a rejection is never anything personal. All that a rejection means is that your work is not right for the publisher. There is no reason to feel as if the publisher is demeaning you or your efforts.

There are plenty of authors who have to submit different works multiple times before they get a successful response. This is something that can be frustrating, and it can take quite some time before you get the response that you are after.

Simply stay calm and make sure that you know how you are presenting yourself. A good reputation as someone who is reliable and easy to work with is something that can help you stay on top of things. It can get you more work, and it can get your existing work acknowledged.

However, behaving badly can also have consequences. You can generally assume that if you behave badly, you will quickly have a reputation that can shut doors in front of you.

Remember, always be courteous, and always be professional. It only takes a little bit of work to ruin a reputation, and it takes a lot of work to build one back up from a flaming ruin.

If you worry that you have offended, send a sincere email off to the offended party, state that you were wrong without equivocating, and promise to do better.

There is no guarantee that it will work, but you can rest content understanding that you have done everything in your power to fix the faux pas in question. It is always better to do what you can.

Chapter 9) Vanity Publishing

Vanity publishing is the process where you pay a firm or company to turn your words into books. Vanity publishing has some problems when it comes to getting your words out there, but you will find that if you simply know what you are doing, you are going to be in much better shape. Learn about what vanity publishing is, and how you can make it work for you.

1) What Does a Vanity Press Do?

A vanity press can actually span several services. Some services do nothing but print your book for you. You will negotiate with them regarding what you want the book to look like, you provide them with images for the cover or the interior, and you are the one who determines whether it is a paperback, a trade paperback or a hardcover. You will likely have to commit to a minimum order, and you will be paying for a straightforward exchange.

Some vanity presses offer marketing services as well. They usually offer a graduated table of fees, where they will put out a certain amount of press for your book and do their part to get your books into bookstores. Remember that no matter what they promise, their efforts are going to be less efficient and less capable than what is offered by professional presses.

Finally, there are luxury vanity presses that offer very beautiful, very limited numbers of books. You provide them with the text or a printed copy of the work, and they will turn your book into a leather bound work of art. These services are quite expensive, but the result is gorgeous.

2) Who Should Work With Vanity Publishers?

When you are someone who is invested in getting your work into a print and bound format, vanity publishing might be for you. However, before you go to invest in vanity publishing, there are a few things that you need to consider.

Who should publish with a vanity press?

The first thing to realize is that a vanity press does not guarantee that you will make any money from your book. If you are comfortable with your work simply existing rather than going out to make you money, vanity publishing is just fine.

For example, if you are writing an account of your family's history and you are just planning to hand out copies to the family members that are important to you, vanity publishing is perfect. You can pay a fee to have ten to a hundred books run off, and you can give them as gifts or save them for your personal library.

Vanity publishing is also perfect when you are someone who has a lot of skills when it comes to marketing. One of the reasons to do vanity publishing is because you prefer to be in control of everything, from the cover design to the page layout to the marketing choices.

Vanity publishing puts you in charge of these things, but that means that you absolutely need to be on top of them. The only way that you can even breakeven through vanity publishing is essentially by being a one-person publishing industry.

3) Services to Consider

A vanity press will offer many services to you regarding your work. It is up to you to decide which of these services that you need.

For example, many vanity presses offer editing and formatting help for new writers. Remember that editing and formatting are skilled tasks, and if you have no experience with them, it is often worth your while to take someone up on these services.

Some other services include finding you an illustrator and still others involve marketing, sales, and advertising.

Remember that vanity publishing services run the gamut from a bare bones deal where you will get very plain copies of your books to very elaborate setups where you get services that are very similar to those offered by a real publishing house.

Remember, however, that where dealing with a conventional publishing house is like selling your work, a vanity press is essentially you investing your own novel.

Instead of the publishing company investing in you, you are investing yourself. You need to have a budget that you are using to create a book that you want to see produced, and you are taking on the burden of publishing it and sending it around, whether you are doing it yourself or paying others to do it.

4) What You Need to Know

Across the board, vanity publishers make their money off of authors. Their investment is in making sure that you purchase their services, not in selling your book.

This can make a world of difference when you are looking to see how your book will be received and what you can do in order to get it out in the world.

There is nothing wrong with using vanity presses, but you should be aware of what they are doing, and how they are making their money. Be aware of the fact that you will likely be dealing with people who want to up sell you on their services, and whose top priority is getting your money.

5) Should I Publish With a Vanity Press?

It really depends on many factors as to whether you want to deal with a vanity press at all.

For some people, the amount of control that they receive over the process is worth the amount it costs them out of pocket. For other people, who only want a few copies of a family memoir on their shelf, vanity publishing is perfect.

If you are thinking about publishing with a vanity press, take a moment to consider your budget. What are you willing to pay, and what services do you need? Are you ready to be firm when it comes to negotiation, and are you ready to stop negotiations if you feel that you are being pressured?

These are all important things to consider. If you want to make money off of a text that you have had published with a vanity publisher, be willing to be your own advocate. You will definitely realize that you need to be a great businessperson when you are doing this.

6) Warnings

Vanity publishing is something that definitely has its fair share of stigma in the publishing world. There are definitely vanity publishers out there who give you your money's worth, but the truth is that there is a long history of companies that are simply looking to make money off of gullible writers.

If you are worried about having people take advantage of you, there are a few things to watch out for.

Be very wary of services that make extravagant promises. If they say that they can shoot you to the top of a bestseller list while allowing you to keep all of the profits to yourself, they are lying.

Also remember that people who are vague about what they will do for you are usually trying to pull something. A good vanity publisher is one that is very honest about what it offers. If there are a lot of vague promises, consultancy services and a bill that just seems to keep growing and growing, be aware that you may be looking at people who just want to make money at your expense.

Be aware of the fact that there are plenty of vanity publishers who have been sued by angry writers in the past. The Science Fiction Writer's Association has reported several that have since closed their doors.

For example, Commonwealth Publications was sued by writers who never received the books that they had published, who were never given the marketing assistance that they were offered, and never received any royalties from books that were actually sold.

Another publisher, Press-Tige, swindled almost a million dollars from more than 200 authors. Press-Tige was masterminded by a single person named Martha Ivery, who also masqueraded as a literary agent who acted as a liaison between the authors and the so-called publisher. At first the publisher behaved much like a normal vanity publisher, though delays were common and contracts poorly maintained. Finally, services and contracts were sold, but no work was actually done, and Ivery ended up in prison.

The risks of vanity publishing can be quite high, and you must always know what you are getting yourself into. No matter where you choose to publish your novel, you will discover that people want to make money off of it. Conventional publishers make money off of the sale of the books, and vanity publishers make money off of you.

7) The Middle Ground

In recent years, there have been a number of services that cross the boundary between vanity publishers and self-publishing, as described in the next chapter. These services can be very helpful if you are looking at self-publishing but lack some of the important knowledge.

When you are looking into self-publishing but you do not know how to do things like edit your work, format it for a number of different platforms or how to get it onto Amazon, these publishers can step in.

These publishers are very firm about what they do and do not handle, and they are also very upfront about the fees that they might collect. For example, some limited services only offer formatting help for a fixed fee. These services do not take royalties from you down the line, nor do they have any recurring fees attached.

There are also services that offer you some marketing services, but only in exchange for royalties, though this package is usually bundled with other services.

If you are considering this form of self-publishing, be willing to consider how this might work for you. Vanity publishers do have a lot to do with the industry, and in many cases, they have skills that benefit you. However, you must always be aware of what you are paying for and how you can proceed.

8) Vanity Publishing Stigma

Another thing that you need to consider is that vanity publishing has a bit of a stigma attached to it. This means that some conventional publishers take it as a negative factor when a writer who is submitting to them has vanity published in the past.

If you ever want to continue your work in the conventional writing field, you should consider what this might mean for your prospects. To many conventional publishers, vanity publishing is a sign of an amateur.

This is of course not a concern if you are invested in staying with vanity publishing and self-publishing throughout your writing career. However, although there have been a few writers who have leveraged a career in vanity publishing into a career with professional publishing, the chances of doing so are vanishingly small, and the people who have managed this feat have been both very, very talented and very, very lucky.

If you decide to go ahead with your vanity publishing while considering a career with professional publishers, take a moment to think about how you can present yourself. If your vanity publishing has made little money, it is not worth mentioning at all when you present yourself to a publisher.

However, if your vanity publishing has enjoyed some moderate success, like high sales on Amazon, some local awards, or some other kind of renown, it is possible that you can use this to get the attention of a publisher or an agent.

9) A Final Word on Vanity Publishing

Vanity publishing can be a risky field for a number of reasons, and one thing that makes it harder is the perception that vanity publishing is something that is simply engaged in by people who are amateurs or who are not good enough to have their work published otherwise.

There is nothing at all wrong with engaging in vanity publishing as long as you know exactly what you are doing and why you are doing it.

Make sure that you do not allow a company to take advantage of you, and that you are willing to get the services that you require.

Know what you want and how you are going to get it from the vanity publisher that you choose.

Chapter 10) Self-Publishing

We're living in a brand new era and with lots of self-publishing platforms available online, it has never been easier to publish your own book. Self-publishing puts all of the control squarely in your hands, if you are someone who likes to make sure that everything is taken care of in the right way, this might be for you.

Before you get started with self-publishing, however, there are a few things to be aware of. Are you the right person for this specialized procedure? Do you know how to maintain your momentum?

Self-publishing is the new big thing in the publishing world, but that does not mean that it is easy. Take a moment to figure out how you can make this publishing venture work for you.

When you self-publish, you are your own editor. This can be both terrifying and liberating because you are the only person you answer to regarding the text. This of course means that you need to be as hard on yourself as a professional editor.

When you are self-publishing, they say that there is no such thing as too many edits. Simply sit down and start looking at your manuscript. You are responsible for everything, starting with the periods and commas and ending with the plot holes.

Remember that this will take up a lot of time. Do not expect to be done soon, and make sure that you are getting everything looked at. Get your friends involved or look for editing services. It all definitely pays off.

It is also of crucial importance that you self publish your book in different formats. www.WorldwideSelfpublishing.com by the well-known Internet marketer Christine Clayfield explains all you need to know about self-publishing your book. EVERYTHING is explained from A to Z. All you need to do is watch the video tutorials and apply it to your own book. The end result will be your book all over the world and all over the web in all the formats a reader can read a book.

Surprisingly, for £41 or $67, you can publish your hard copy book and have it distributed all over the world, including listing on all the Amazon sites! Unbelievable but true.

Out of all of the self-publishing products out there, this program is simply the best and there are no puzzle pieces missing. When you've written your book, I highly recommend that you buy the video tutorials from www.worldwideselfpublishing.com

The different forms of publishing are very well explained in the videos and the different companies you can work with if you want to self publish are compared in the videos. You will learn the pro's and con's of several major publishing companies.

1) Digital Forever

There are a few people who self-publish who decide to go with print, but the real joy of self-publication is that you are able to go with digital. There are some services that let you publish your work with a print on demand service, but you should always see what kind of cost that adds to your work. Sometimes, printing costs are not something that you want to add on for your readers, so be wary.

The great thing about digital self-publishing is that you can learn to do it on your own, and it takes very little time.

2) Formatting

Formatting a self-published work is actually very simple. All you really need is a word processor, and if you have been writing for a while, you already have that.

Remember that your document should be saved as .doc or a docx as well as .htm or .html. This allows you to upload your work easily and without any problem to Amazon and other digital marketplaces. Both the .doc and .html format have their own strengths, and if you have both, you can upload wherever you like. Some people find that it is most convenient to do all of their editing in .doc and then to save everything as .html later on.

An important tip is that you should not do anything manually. There was a time when hitting Tab every time you wanted to indent a paragraph was fine, but now that can actually mess with the way your book looks.

Instead, get comfortable with page styles, which are located under the Format menu, and then the Styles section in Word. Highlight a chunk of text, give it the relevant style, and then, if necessary, right-click the text to edit the style. This may feel clunky if you are someone who is used to doing everything manually, but it pays off in the end!

The styles section is where you will choose things like the spacing between lines, the length of the indents, the font and the font sizes.

If you want to stick with something very general, set your page style to be double-spaced with .5 inch indents using 12 pt Times New Roman. This is very generalized, but highly functional.

When you are dealing with your page set up, start from the largest unit and work your way in. For example, if you are doing a standard book size, go into the Page Layout menu and choose 6 x 11, which is a standard size used by sites like Lulu and Amazon.

Remember to keep your margins very large and clear. Each margin should be at least one inch wide, with plenty of professional books having more.

In the page layout menu, you can choose to make sure that the entire text is justified, meaning that the text is smooth and even on both sides. This is a stylistic choice, but it does make for a tidier look.

Once you have the basic formatting set up, you can deal with everything else.

3) The Cover

Do you need a cover for a self-published book? Though the technical answer is no, the actual answer is a resounding yes. When people browse Amazon, you want their eyes to catch on your book's image, and that is generally the cover.

You do not need to design your own cover, you can outsource that part: outsourcing is explained from A to Z in the videos on www.worldwideselfpublishing.com

When you are looking for a great cover for your book, look at the other covers out there. Look at where the text goes and how the image is centered. Remember that a strong contrast between the title and the cover itself is ideal, and that you must always be willing to spend money on good art.

It is definitely one thing if you are an artist or a graphic designer yourself. If you have worked or spent time in these fields, there is nothing stopping you from designing your own cover.

However, if you do not have any graphic experience, it is entirely worth your while to bring in a professional. Look for a graphic designer who is looking to build their portfolio and who would love a chance to do covers.

You can choose from traditionally painted covers, digital art covers, or composite covers that are made from a store of different online images.

When working with a good graphic design artist, be willing to communicate what you want. They may not necessarily read the work, so be ready with a few pages you want them to read or a detailed description of what you are looking for.

Good art is something that should be paid for. Do not ask someone to do the work for the exposure or for a share of the profits. Instead, discuss a flat fee for the work, negotiate for what rights you want and what rights you don't mind them keeping, and be willing to put up a deposit that is around half the cost of the work at the very beginning.

4) Front Matter

The front matter is everything that goes into your book between the cover and the start of the text. Although having front matter is not strictly necessary when it comes to self-published works, it is a good idea to have it. It makes your work look more professional, and it is customary.

When you are creating a self-published book, the front matter usually proceeds with the title page, the copyright page, the acknowledgments, and the table of contents, if there are any.

If you want an idea of what these things look like, just flip open any book you have close to hand.

After the title page, if you have written any other books, you may choose to have them mentioned here.

Do not copy a standard copyright statement off of a book. You want to create one for yourself, and the process is quite simple. You begin with a copyright symbol, the word "copyright," followed by your name, the date, and the phrase "All Rights

Reserved."

An example of a basic copyright statement might look like this:

© Copyright Jane Doe 2014 All Rights Reserved

Many people also include the phrase "No part of this document may be reproduced without written consent from the author."

When making your acknowledgments page, just keep it simple and heart-felt. This is a simple statement, and there will be a place for further thanks later on in the book.

A Table of Contents is like any other table, and can be found by going to the Insert menu in Windows and locating the Indexes and Tables option. Then you will be guided into creating a Table of Contents that will update itself as you add or remove from the document.

5) End Matter

Just like front matter is what goes in front of your text, end matter is what at the end. In general, it feels more complete and more professional to leave a few blank pages in the back even if you don't want anything else there.

However, the end matter area is a good place for other content that does not fit anywhere else. If your work has an appendix or an index, it would go here. An author's biography should also go here, as can any thanks you might want to give to people who have helped you along the way.

Your author's biography is where you have a chance to tell people about yourself. This is a great place to let people know what else you are working on and any other information that they might want to know.

The general rule about biographies for books is that you want to keep it short, inoffensive and still relevant to you. Write in the third person, and if it fits with your work, feel free to get a little playful with it. Talk a little bit about your life, your past jobs, and the other things you do as well as being a writer. You can close with some other works that you are considering.

After you get all of that taken care of, and the document saved, you are on your way!

6) Uploading

The best place to upload your work is Amazon, though Smashwords, PubIt and Kindle Direct Publishing are all other alternatives. Remember that you should always check the terms and find out what kind of fees might be taken out. Some operate free of charge, and others will ask for a percentage of your sales.

Uploading a book for publishing is also explained in www.worldwideselfpublishing.com

Each site has specific rules and requirements for your manuscript, so read carefully and make sure that you know what you are in for.

Self-Promotion

When you are with a publishing house, no matter how small, they will do some promotion for you. If you are self-publishing, you will find that you have to do it on your own.

First, make sure that you have a social media presence. Even if you do not intend to use Twitter, Facebook, and Tumblr, acquire the ones under your name if at all possible. It will save confusion later on.

Set up a website. This enables people to find you on the web if they need to. As a writer, your website needs to be competent, but it does not need to be flashy. Look up a basic Wordpress format and simply go from there.

Find out the kind of self-promotion that works for you. Whatever social media you are on, announce your work. Now is not the time to be shy. Do not gum up the works by saying that the work is not very good or pointing out the flaws. Just let people know that the work is there and that they should take a look at it if they want to.

One great way to connect with fans is to write a blog. Ideally, the best time to create a blog is as you are writing the book, but if you did not, there is no time like the present to start. When running a blog, talk about your book, the things that went into making it, and your life in general. People get invested when they can learn more about the person who is doing the writing.

Be creative if you want to be. If you are someone who loves things like trailers and you have the skills, consider making a trailer for your book for YouTube. Create contests and give away free copies, or do an Ask Me Anything on Reddit. Find the kind of advertising that works for you, and remember that if you are not comfortable, there is a good chance that everyone can tell.

7) Should I Do a Book Tour?

Book tours are something that we have all heard about, but unless you are a very popular writer with a real fan following, you should skip the tour unless you already happen to be in the area and meeting with fans. Book tours are really only publicity for full-time professional writers with a staff at their disposal. Setting up your own book tour is often time consuming and takes away from time you could be using to write.

In addition to that, it's pretty heartbreaking when you show up for your signing but no one else does. Unless someone is arranging a book tour for you and fairly certain that you are going to get a turn out, give this a pass.

To end the self-publishing section, I am repeating here what I already said before.

It is also of crucial importance that you self publish your book in different formats. www.WorldwideSelfpublishing.com by the well-known Internet marketer Christine Clayfield, explains all you need to know about self publishing your book. EVERYTHING is explained from A to Z. All you need to do is watch the video tutorials and apply it to your own book.

Out of all the self-publishing products out there, this program is simply the best and there are no puzzle pieces missing. When you've written your book, I highly recommend that you buy the video tutorials from www.worldwideselfpublishing.com

Chapter 11) General Tips

Writing is a very personal thing, and you may find that it takes you a lot of time and effort to get some traction. These are some tips that can keep you going if you are not sure how well your work is going and what you need to do.

1) Do Other Things

Writing is a process where you take the contents of your brain, dump it out, and put it on a piece of paper or on the screen for other people to see. This is something that can take a lot of time, and there is nothing wrong with being a slow writer.

However, if you don't have anything in your brain to write about, you are going to end up a lot more frustrated than you thought possible!

When you are staring at the screen and you cannot decide what your characters are going to do next, take a moment to think about what needs to happen. If nothing is coming, move on to something else.

It does not matter what else you are doing. Whether you have decided to learn to sew, to cook a dish that has always interested you, to make sure that your dogs have the exercise they need, or to learn the basics of Aramaic, you are doing something that can feed your brain.

Part of being a professional writer is not allowing yourself to get stuck. Remember that your brain needs to be fed on a regular basis. You cannot expect it to continue to produce content if you are having issues with feeding it!

Do things that enrich you or that interest you. You do not have to stick with high culture events like classical concerts or museums unless you want to. Go to a place that makes you feel passionate, or that soothes you, or where you feel excited.

2) Write Something Else

When you are writing a long work, you need to make sure that you keep your focus. You should never get so distracted with things that you run off to start a brand new project!

There are too many writers out there with several half-finished novels that are never going to go anywhere, and the result is that their writing stalls out early and easily.

However, even though you are committed to a longer work, remember that you can derail for a while just to take a break. If you are working on something long and very serious, you will discover that simply having something lighter going on the side can help.

If you are a poet as well as a writer, take some time to write a poem. Write a short story, or try writing in the style of someone that you admire.

Different kinds of writing can help you feel a lot more competent and accomplished when you get back to your own work. This is a good trick if you have been stuck for a while and you are not sure how to proceed.

Come back to your main work when you are done, but if you are not making any progress, try distracting yourself with another form of writing. This can give you a new appreciation of other genres, and it can help you figure out how to move forward with the writing that you are struggling with.

Remember to make the time to speak with your family and friends. Writing is a consuming job, and because it is very encompassing and it can be hard to bring the people that you love into it.

When you need a break, go find the people who love you and spend some time with them. If they are feeling a little neglected, remember that you should be balancing your time a little more effectively.

3) Write What You Love

You've heard the adage that you should always write what you know, but another thing to consider is that you should write what you love.

The sad thing is that there is a lot of prejudice about different kinds of writing. Some people feel that literary fiction is far superior to any sort of genre fiction, or that science fiction is all about aliens and guns. Some people think that romance is silly or illegitimate or that mysteries are all the same.

If you think this, stop it at once.

Life is too short not to write the things that make you happy, and life is also too short to judge different types of literature against some arbitrary checklist. If it exists, someone wants to read it.

When you want to write something, whether you think it is silly or it is in a genre that other people do not respect, write it. A great story is a great story no matter what genre it is in.

At the very bottom of it all is experience. If you love a genre, you have likely read a lot of it. That makes you an expert simply through proximity. You know how the genre works, you know what people think and feel about it, and you know what makes a great story.

Do not try to fit your work into a genre that you don't really like or enjoy. It is one thing to feel as if your work is changing and needs something new, and to explore new areas, but if you do not enjoy reading the thing that you are writing, there is something wrong!

4) Eye Breaks

If you are a writer, you are going to be using your eyes a lot. You will spend a lot of your time focusing on a computer screen, and although you should always spend time working, remember to give your eyes a break as well!

The problem that many people face is that their eyes often get strained. If you work an office job, there is a good chance that you spend hours of every day looking at a computer screen. Then you come home and spend even more hours looking at the screen as you work on your novel.

Your eyes need a break, so make sure that on a regular basis, you look away from the screen. Focus on something that is far away for a few moments before looking back at your screen. If you know how to touch type, you do not even have to stop work to do so.

Take care of your eyes, and get regular exams. There are programs that can help you type if your eyes start to go, but it is far better to save your sight while you can.

5) Hand Breaks

You use your hands every day, and sometimes, you can really tell! Your hands handle a huge amount of fine manipulation over the course of the day, and as a result, you will find that they can end up quite sore.

When you want to preserve your hands as a writer, first know your limits. You will always need to use them more, so make sure that you know how much you want to work on a given day. Some writers have minimum word counts, but other writers have maximum word counts.

If you find that your hands are hurting after a full day at the keyboard, limit the amount of works that you can do in a day. If you feel sore at 8,000 words, cut back to 5,000. If you feel bad at 5,000 words, cut back to 2,000.

You may have a lot of words to get out there, but it is far better to save your hands. If you have the capability to do so, you can also look up a speech to text program where you can get words onto the page simply by speaking them.

Another thing for you to consider when you are looking at getting a lot of writing done is hand exercises. One great hand exercise taken from the deaf community is to move your hands through the positions for the sign for the letter "E" to the sign for the letter "C."

You form the sign for E by curling your fingertips down to touch the spot where they hit the palm. Tuck your thumb against your palm and arch your hand back a little.

Move your hand from this position to the C position, where you simply curl your fingers and your thumb as if you were wrapping them around a cup, forming a C out of your hand.

Moving from the E position to the C position loosens up muscles that are tight from a lot of work.

Another thing for you to try is to use one hand to bend your palm back for ten seconds, and then to do the same with your fingers. Bending your muscles backwards allows you to keep a full range of mobility when you are getting stiff.

6) Ergonomics

If you are a writer, you are going to be spending a lot of time at your desk. While spending some time hunched over the laptop at the couch, or curled up on the floor can be fun, you need a good desk and chair situation.

Firstly, remember that you should not crane your head to look up at your screen, and nor should you turn your head to look down at it. Instead, the screen should be across from your face, and your ability to see it should be in as direct a line as possible.

Secondly, look at how you are sitting. The general rule to remember is that your body should be at a series of 90-degree angles. Your feet should be flat on the floor and your legs should be at a ninety-degree angle to the ground. Your knees should be bent at 90-degree angles, and if you are sitting at a chair that is neither too high nor too low, this will work.

The bend between your torso and your lap should be a 90-degree angle as well. This means that you should not slide back in your chair, and you should not bend forward in order to see the screen.

Your chair should be comfortable for you. It should connect with your back from the base of your spine up to your shoulders at least, and if it is uncomfortable, you need to do something about it!

Good ergonomics will keep you healthy across the board, and if you are someone who is willing to put a little bit of time and investment into your desk setup, you will be a lot happier.

7) Avoiding Distractions

Part of good writing is simply getting yourself into the chair, and this is where having an easily distracted mind can hurt you. Sometimes, it seems like the minute you sit down to write, you remembered that you need to mail off some checks or an old friend calls you up for some fun.

You should not avoid the pleasures of life, but neither should you work in a way that does not allow you get the words on the page. Do what you need to do to avoid distractions, whether that means refusing to move from the desk for an hour or doing your work when everyone else is asleep.

When you write, you need to avoid distractions. You can shut the cat out of the room, and you can wait until the kids are asleep, but the Internet is one of the worst distractions out there.

It's a tough call to make. If you are doing a story that requires a lot of research, the Internet is a fabulous resource. However, how can you draw the line between using the Internet to help you move forward and using the Internet to help you waste time?

One way to make sure that the Internet does not get in your way is to use a nanny program. These programs stop you from using certain sites at certain times. They will put up a block when you try to access the sites, and they may play a loud noise to punish you.

These programs are easily disabled, but that is not the point. If you really want to get to your favorite news sites, you certainly will, but the blocking program makes you think about it before you can really do it.

Use one of these programs to make sure that you do not waste all of the precious time that you have decided to devote to writing.

You will at least have to consider what you are doing before you commit to getting lost on the Internet.

8) Read Your Dialogue Out Loud

One of the best things about writing is that you get to say all of those things that you have only thought. When a character is as frustrated as you are, you can go off on other characters the way that you can't in real life.

However, how can you make sure that your dialogue flows? Bad dialogue clunks hard, and it can actually ruin someone's suspension of disbelief.

If you are someone who has not had a lot of experience in writing dialogue, the best thing that you can do is to start listening. Listen to the people around you, and listen to the way that they talk.

This is something that can help you pick up other people's speech patterns, and it can allow you to really make the right choices when it comes to dialogue.

If you are uncertain whether some dialogue is the right choice for you, you will find that reading it out loud can be quite important. Simply sit with your work and start reading the dialogue out loud, as if you were reading a play.

Skip the exposition, just read the conversation as if there were several characters in the room who are chatting with one another. Doing this will give you an idea if the writing is clear or if it is something that needs to be tailored.

As you read your own dialog out loud, watch out for word choice, and of course be willing to change things. You never know until you do this what might sound odd, or what might be interrupting the flow of the story.

If you are still not certain, consider calling in some friends to help. Hand them your manuscript and simply ask them to read as if they were auditioning for a play. As they do this, listen to them and find out how they are doing.

If they are having trouble with the flow of the words, and if they are stumbling over the way the words fit together, you will find that it is time to go back to the drawing board.

9) Timed Writing Practice

When you are having issues with getting the words on the page, one great exercise to try is to create a typing session for yourself. Some people use this as a way to prepare for the day, while other people simply use this to loosen up their fingers.

Set your clock for five minutes, and then start typing. While you should definitely try to get some material for your story, remember that you do not necessarily need to type anything at all. The goal of the exercise is simply to type for five minutes straight. No matter what the words are, just keep them coming!

This is something that can be very hard at first, especially if you are someone who is feeling nervous about making sure that every word is perfect, but the truth of the matter is that this can help you loosen up.

No matter how uncomfortable it is, simply sit down and make sure that you are getting words typed into your computer. These can be real sentences or they might simply be gibberish. It does not matter, as this exercise is all about loosening up and getting some of the thoughts out of your head.

After you are done, shake out your hands and read what you wrote. You may be surprised to see some interesting material there, or things that you were not aware of writing.

This type of writing can teach you a lot regarding your own process and the way that you work.

10) What Do Your Characters Want?

When you are working on plotting your novel, it is always worth asking yourself what your characters want. Some people have some real issues getting their characters to go out and do things, and the answer to character motivations is always desire.

Think about what your characters want and how they function. Then, as you figure things out, make it difficult to get what they want.

It sounds simple, but every fiction narrative is based on desire. Sometimes the desire is as complex as saving a country from an evil dictator. In other situations, the desire is as simple as surviving the night.

Think about your favorite stories and ask what was motivating the characters. If nothing is motivating them, there is no reason for them to do the things that you want them to do.

When you know what your characters want most, one way to get a plot going is to take it away from them! If you have characters but no novel, this is the way to go.

11) Regarding Your Reviews

No matter how you get your work published, remember that you should always be ready for reviews. Everyone gets them, and no matter how good you are at what you do, you are not going to please everyone.

The first bad review you ever get can feel a lot like a punch in the gut. You may feel angry or hurt, but do remember that reviews are not personal. They are just someone's opinion, and your first bad review, just like your first rejection, will not be the last.

Remember that you are under no obligation to respond to the review. There is no rule that says that you have to engage with the reviewer, and there is nothing that says that you can't just ignore them.

As a matter of fact, most writers have a standing rule not to engage with their reviewers, whether they are good or bad. Some post links to every review, whether good or bad on their blog, while other people stay out of it entirely.

Come up with a strategy that works for you, and stick with it. You do not need to sit and stew with a bad review, and it is always a bad idea to engage a reviewer.

One exception might be made for when a review has gotten something factually wrong. If that is the case, a simple correction on your own space might be all that is necessary.

Authors who respond badly to their own reviews is the stuff of Internet legend, so do not fall into this trap. This is simply a space where you cannot win. Do not fall into a trap where you allow a reviewer to make you angrier and angrier. The only thing that will happen is that you will be mocked and that your reputation will suffer.

Your great reviews are an awesome thing, but remember that you will get bad ones, and that you need to know how you are planning on dealing with them.

12) The Media Diet

If you are an omnivorous reader, this can work for you as often as it works against you. You read a lot, and you have a lot of things to say, and in many cases, you will find yourself enjoying a lot of different things from a lot of different writers.

However, the place where this starts to work against you is when you sit down to write your own work. Suddenly, in the middle of writing your fantasy novel or your memoir, you realize that you want to write a cozy mystery!

The problem with being a writer is that you can really write whatever you want. You can start having fun with mysteries, you can write your own life story, you can record the life of your grandmother and turn it into an epic, and the only real problem is that you cannot do it all at once!

If you are someone who constantly gets attacked by new ideas, you will learn that sometimes, reading things that are out of genre can actually harm your writing efficiency.

This is where the media diet comes in. When you sit down to write your novel, limit yourself in terms of what you can read and watch. For example, if you are writing a book on medieval Europe, make sure that you skip reading mystery novels or watching histories about World War II.

This is not easy if you are someone who reads and consumes media like they breathe, but in many cases, you will find that it can keep you focused on what you are looking at, and it can aid you in your progress.

On top of that, it can make you hurry up and finish your novel if you have something that you desperately want to read, but do not want to break your "diet!"

13) Know Your Genre

One thing that you will hear over and over again is that good writers read. More importantly than that, good writers are people who read and who then ask questions about what they have experienced!

For example, consider how you read a book. There is nothing wrong with reading a book and simply enjoying the experience. That is the way that most people enjoy their books, after all.

However, you will become a better writer and a better reader as well when you start asking yourself the important question of "why?"

For example, why did the hero have to win the fight in the way he or she won it? Why did the villain take this action?

In many ways, when you become a questioning reader, you become someone who can see "backstage" in a novel. You will start to see the decisions that the writer made, and more than that, you can decide if you agree with them or not.

Start asking yourself why stories are told in a certain way. Sometimes there are good reasons to the way that things are done, but in some cases, you will simply find that that they are done that way because they have always been done that way.

Reading constructively will also give you a better idea of how to make your own stories work. People are always interested in novelty, and if you are someone who is very invested in getting attention and showing people something new, you still have to have an idea of where the genre is coming from.

If you want to write something, you should read everything that you can that pertains to it. Some people think that this only makes them derivative, but the truth is that it can only help you. It shows you where you are coming from, where your own readers are going to be coming from and where you can go from there.

As you start learning more and more about yourself as a writer, you will also learn a lot about yourself as a reader as well. This is something that can change the way you look at your favorite books.

14) Respond

You will likely get some messages about your work. One of the best things about writing is that you get to reach out and to talk to people about the writing that you have done and the story that you are telling.

Do not feel overwhelmed if you get fan mail. Remember that these are people who are interested in talking to you or letting you know that you did something that touched them in some way.

There will be some people who miss the point, some people who love your work, some people who love it for all of the wrong reasons and some people who have some questions that you cannot answer.

No matter what, every positive inquiry should get a response. It does not have to be long, and it does not have to be detailed, but it is always kind to write to the people who have taken the time to write to you. This is something that spreads good will, and you never know when it is going to make a big difference regarding who finds your work.

15) Get Traffic To Your Book.

If you don't tell people that your book is out there, you won't get any sales.

No doubt, Facebook, Twitter and other social media platforms are ideal to get people to talk about your book.

You need to send traffic to your book. This means, once your book is published, you need to let people know that they can buy it.
In the book "**From Newbie To Millionaire**" are over 100 traffic methods, well worth reading. Just search for the book on Amazon. It is written by Christine Clayfield, an internet marketer who has self published over 80 books.

Now that you've finished reading this book, why not read From Newbie To Millionaire, you will learn a lot about the internet and as you know, the internet is the future therefore as a book writer and publisher you do need to know about the power of the internet and how it can help you sell more books.

I've learned a lot from Christine Clayfield and I have achieved a lot by applying what she does in the internet environment and the publishing environment. She has given me a full time income and thanks to her, I have been able to say goodbye to my boss! I am forever grateful to her and I promised her that I would promote her products, which is why I recommend her products in this book.
On top of that, I always wanted to write a book about how to write a book so I have killed two birds with one stone by writing and publishing this book.

This book was published following Christine Clayfield's publishing method. You've found the book and bought it so that is proof her publishing methods work.

I hope this book has been helpful to you and I wish you good luck with getting your book finished and more importantly, published.

Vivian Venfield

Lightning Source UK Ltd.
Milton Keynes UK
UKOW04f1956240214

227071UK00013B/264/P